A Glimpse of Greatness

EMPEROR HAILE SELASSIE I: THE PERSON

Abebe Ambatchew

Trafford
PUBLISHING™

Order this book online at www.trafford.com
or email orders@trafford.com

Most Trafford titles are also available at major online book retailers.

© Copyright 2009 Abebe Ambatchew.
All rights reserved. No part of this publication may be reproduced, stored in a retrieval
system, or transmitted, in any form or by any means, electronic, mechanical, photocopying,
recording, or otherwise, without the written prior permission of the author.

Note for Librarians: A cataloguing record for this book is available from Library
and Archives Canada at www.collectionscanada.ca/amicus/index-e.html

Printed in Victoria, BC, Canada.

ISBN: 978-1-4251-5306-9 (sc)
ISBN: 978-1-4251-5307-6 (e-book)

*Our mission is to efficiently provide the world's finest, most comprehensive
book publishing service, enabling every author to experience success.
To find out how to publish your book, your way, and have it available
worldwide, visit us online at www.trafford.com*

 www.trafford.com

North America & international
toll-free: 1 888 232 4444 (USA & Canada)
phone: 250 383 6864 ♦ fax: 812 355 4082

Dedication

This book is dedicated to all those who helped build a better Ethiopia and the young who hoped for an even better country but who were, without justice, killed by the military regime, the Dergue, in prisons, streets, and even in their homes in front of their parents or children.

Contents

Preface i

Acknowledgements v

Introduction vii

1 Father and Son 1

2 Claim and Rise to Power 10

3 The Education Emperor 18

 Christmas Gifts and Prizes 20

 The Sidamo Eight Go Imperial 24

 A Little Girl Meets the Emperor 26

 The Skinny Boy Flexes His Muscles 27

 Initial Hurdles to the Introduction of Education 29

 Let Them Go East Too 30

 Royal Attention for the Girls 31

 A Guest for All Occasions 32

4 A Prized Experience 34

 The Early Days of the Prize Trust 35

 No Veto on Award Nominees 41

 No Award by Petition 45

 The Nobel Prospect 47

and we watched its decline. I was motivated to write about him not because I was a trusted government official with special access to have insights in how he governed, but rather because I had the rare opportunity to see him more as an individual than the head of state. In fact, I did not serve in the established government structure but in chartered institutions. My assignment as head of a private organization, the Haile Selassie I Prize Trust, that he set up with his funds gave me, in addition to information I gathered from former senior officials, such an opportunity. My encounters with him, and with those around him were invaluable experiences that should be shared and become part of the record of the Emperor's rule.

It is incumbent on those who knew and dealt with the Emperor, albeit in varying degrees, to share their perceptions and experiences to enable a better understanding of this great leader. It is fortunate that some, like former ministers and officials have ably done so. This is not to say that presentations, mine included, will be free from some personal biases, positive or negative. The Emperor had after all his share of those who liked him very much or hated him intensely. He was fair and proper in his dealings with me even at the time of a strained separation from the Haile Selassie I Prize Trust.[1] In this book, I have tried to share my experiences as objectively as possible.

What follows does not focus on his reign, or even on his remarkable political ascendancy. Such aspects were touched upon to the extent that they shed light on his personality and individualism. My limited objective is to share a few eyewitness accounts and personal impressions of the Emperor in order to give a fuller sense of Haile

---

1 Two years after I joined the Prize Trust, I requested release to go back to the university because of the distracting land disputes and my conviction that they will lead to an unpleasant separation. I was aware of pressure being exerted on the Emperor by officials involved in the disputes and who had claims against the Trust. He did not like my request and flatly said no. I was asked to hand over my responsibilities two years later. I welcomed the decision with quiet relief. The Emperor saw me a month after I left the Trust and instructed that my wish be respected with regard to a new assignment. And it was respected in full. I got the clear impression that he did not feel comfortable with his decision. I learnt from Abebe Kebede that he did express so.

Selassie I, the person. Even in this task, coverage was confined to first-hand recollections that the writer and some of his close contemporaries have of the Emperor.

Specific events and information from personal experiences could provide some insights about the Emperor and the environment within which he operated. The events and incidents cited certainly gave me a better appreciation of some of his efforts, failings, and of him as a person.

My mixed feelings of admiration and skepticism shifted over the years, and I came to see the Emperor as a pragmatic and tough individual of courage, faith, and openness to new ideas. At the same time, I found to be valid criticisms such as being unduly influenced by contrary advice, reluctance to appreciate and accept the reality of aging, and the failure to depersonalize politics and reduce adequately his role as the center of power as valid.

Many of the educated excepting those who held senior positions in government or those who, as was my case, came in contact with him because of the nature of their assignments, had very limited opportunities to come to know him as a person. In spite of the contention that it was impossible to know him anyway, even with significant access to him, I believe my limited but direct exposure to him enabled me and those who had similar exposure to him to know him as a complex and exceptional individual. I also saw him with the eyes of a novice to the Palace environment and as one who was relatively free of the biases developed, for or against, because of long association and service under a leader.

The anecdotes cited in this book reveal, among other things, the Emperor's very human and even amusing side, his unwavering commitment especially to the expansion of education, bias for the educated, and his receptiveness to new ideas. Cumulatively, incidents could be indicative of the person and character. Incidents presented in the manner they occurred give the reader human touch and a concrete basis to make his or her judgment.

I have highlighted facts and substance rather than focus on the individuals involved. Names are therefore indicated only where the individual was involved in an official capacity or where the mention of the name did not reflect on the individual. This is especially true about the individuals involved in the land disputes of the Prize Trust. It would be unfair to characterize the persons involved on the basis of limited contexts or single incidents.

The Emperor was known as a man who could instill fear and generate hatred but, more often, a man who earned loyalty and respect. He was a strong man, a "born leader," who skillfully, and albeit conservatively, moved Ethiopia to incremental progress and recognition. He worked hard to harmonize modernization with the heritage of greatness, and aspirations of Ethiopia as the country struggled through decades of evolution and slow change.

Acknowledgements

I am greatly indebted to many people who have contributed to my effort with advice, specific inputs in the form of stories on incidents, comments, and reading material. No less was valuable the constant encouragement I received from all those who came to know about my project. I have been amazed by the high level of interest they showed in the subject of the Emperor and the unhappiness they felt about the biased and adverse treatment he and those who served under his leadership have received. At the risk of leaving some deserving people out, I express my profound thanks and gratitude to many who helped in diverse ways:

Dr. Adem Abdallah, Ato Bekele Beshah, Ato Beruk Bekele, Engineer Demissie Abebe, Ato Gorfu Gebre Medhin, Ato Hailu Gebre Hiwot, Ambassador Hailu Wolde Emanuel, Ato Kibreye Dejene, H.E. Ato Ketema Yifru, H.E. Ato Paulos Asrat, H.E. Ato Tekle Tsadik Mekuria, Ato Telahun Workeneh, Ato Tibebe Desta and Ato Truesaw Meshesha.

I owe special thanks to Miss Suzan O'Hara for meticulously editing the manuscript and her useful suggestions.

I am most grateful for the unreserved support and understanding of my wife Rahel and my sons Dereje, Dehne and Beruk.

Photographs:
Ato Mulugetta Bekele and Imperial Ministry of Information

Introduction

The episodes described in this book are not all events that I have witnessed or was a part of; they are also stories gathered as first-hand testimony from individuals who had significant direct dealings with the Emperor and whose integrity and judgment I respect. Their stories were often corroborated by other sources. In almost all cases, their encounters with the Emperor had left them with lasting and often positive impressions.

Like thousands of others, my initial exposures with the Emperor were when he visited us on school days and events, when we went to the Palace or Janhoy Meda to receive Christmas gifts, and when I was a boarding student in primary and secondary schools and college. I also witnessed the Emperor at the many formal functions and events over which he presided or was the guest of honor.

My closest and the most important association with him was as the first director of the Haile Selassie Prize Trust, one of the two major foundations the Emperor established with his own money. Although the Emperor was assisting in many humanitarian activities, the first foundation, Haile Selassie I Foundation, was formally established in 1952. This was a humanitarian organization much larger and diverse in its activities than the Prize Trust. Ato Abebe Kebede, a friend from school days, led the Foundation for many years and expanded its reach and resources through additional support and investments. Although both of us had direct contact with the Emperor in matters that dealt with our respective organizations, he had almost daily contact with the Emperor during his many years of service. Abebe was central in the establishment of the Trust and his advice and support with regards to dealings with the Emperor in the early days of my assignment in the Haile Selassie I Prize Trust were indispensable.

The fortuitous assignment in the Prize Trust, a year after my return from graduate studies abroad enabled me to have a glimpse, and it is just a glimpse, of the Emperor more as a person rather than the head of state and the ruler.

My meetings with him consisted of audiences or meetings, some lasting only a few minutes. His visits to the Prize Trust properties were also revealing opportunities where I was able to see the Emperor involved in less formal settings and in development activities close to his heart. Most of the meetings involved disputes related to the land properties given to the Prize Trust. Issues strictly related to the core activities of the awards and scholarships came up only a dozen times during my tenure in the Trust.

The Prize Trust was not, as it was sometimes perceived, a humanitarian foundation. Nor was it a public relations undertaking as some in the Board of Trustees wanted to make it. People also confused it with the Haile Selassie I Foundation. Even the Emperor had to get used to the idea that the two were separate organizations with very different tasks. The Prize Trust was established as an independent chartered entity overseen by a Board of Trustees. A senior Englishman, Dr.G.E.W. Wolstenholme played an important advisory role in the drafting of its charter. It was established to promote excellence in performance and research achievement. The Prize Trust sought to emulate the spirit of recognized award-giving institutions such as the Nobel Foundation; it was understandably modest in scope and adapted to focus on Ethiopia and domestic interests. Its non-political nature was built in the charter, so it had very little to do with the government machinery except in matters related to properties, local administrative and security matters in the areas where the estates were located.

Abebe and I had many opportunities to discuss our experiences and work, and I benefited much from his long experience working under the immediate watch of the Emperor. Abebe was known for his hard work and religious devotion. The Emperor knew him as such, reposed trust in him, and appreciated his dedicated service. There were however some difficult moments in their relationship often due to misinformation. Usually an official passed on wrong information to the Emperor or criticizes Abebe or the Foundation. Abebe then had to correct the Emperor's consequent impressions through frequent audiences. There were occasions when the Emperor, basing his judgment on what he believed credible information, had said harsh words to Abebe. Soon after, the Emperor would call him, conducting business as if nothing had happened. In some instances, he would ask him if the harsh words had hurt his feelings. Such a query was the closest thing to an apology.

Abebe's genuine admiration and respect for the Emperor were so strong that neither intimidation nor threats to his life by the military regime that deposed the Emperor turned Abebe into a false witness. He was pressured to incriminate the Emperor, but he refused. Consequently, Abebe was murdered after several years of imprisonment. As in the case of those officials massacred in November 1974, he was killed along with other highly respected officials such as the Patriarch of the Ethiopian Orthodox Tewahedo Church, Abune Teoflos, the former president of the national university, Ledj Kassa Wolde Mariam, and the minister of education, Ato Seifu Mahteme Sellassie. It is widely believed that Abebe's refusal to support the Dergue's charges was the main factor in his murder.

I hope that this book will help readers to form their own appreciation of Emperor Haile Selassie, the person. It would be a travesty if readers were satisfied with settling to blindly admire or criticize him. Indifference to objectively assessing his role is tantamount to indifference to a very important period of Ethiopian history and the captain who steered the country through it. After all, during this period of the Emperor's reign. Ethiopia fought Italian aggression, earned respected membership in the international community, laid the basis for development, and attained leadership in African politics.

1

Father and Son

People know the public Emperor Hale Selassie I, a name that still evokes an image of a smiling elderly man often dressed in a tan military uniform or, less often, a dark suit waving to large crowds and acknowledging their warm applauses with gentle bows of the head. The older international generation recalled and admired a younger bearded and somber leader pleading at the League of Nations for material help for his country's fight against fascism and reminding the League of its Covenant obligations to collective security and the security of weaker nations. Leaders of the 1945 Yalta Conference met with a discouraged but a quietly determined exile leader, and accorded him deference and admiration at his time of defeat and desperation.

Over the years, his peers praised him glowingly highlighting his long track record in the international arena. The Emperor's support to the United Nations, his leadership role in African unity efforts, and policies that, though pro-western, did not alienate countries with opposed persuasions won him support and proper, if not cordial, relations.

For decades before his deposition by the military, peoples and governments hosted him in their capitals and conferred upon him honorary degrees and awarded him so many medals that he was considered, probably, the "most decorated" leader of his time.

Former President Nelson Mandela who admired the Emperor, though "he did not consider Ethiopia as a model of democracy",

showed warmth and pride when he, in 1962, looked forward to
meeting the Emperor and visiting Ethiopia. He said, "I felt I would
be visiting my own genesis, unearthing the roots of what made me an
African. Meeting the Emperor himself would be like shaking hands
with history."[2]

The international media found throughout the Emperor's reign
something to write about him, often favorably – exile, triumphant
return to his liberated capital, attempted coups, his dignified and yet
dominating presence in capitals of countries. The unique image he
presented and the issues he stood for, from collective security to the
promotion of African Unity, made him a subject of continued interest.

At home, unlike the leaders who followed him, Emperor Haile
Selassie kept a high profile by staying in touch with the people and
participating in unending public functions and visits to development
projects, to institutions and services.

Those of us who lived during his reign have been directly affected
by his consuming interest in our education and careers and cherish
memories of the interactions we had with him. During his visits to
campuses and to students departing for studies abroad, the Emperor
put questions about career plans, especially to the senior students.
He had his preferred areas of study to promote, namely engineering,
medicine, education, and agriculture. He randomly selected students
and asked what career choices they have made and what particular
benefits the choices would bring to the country.

I look back with amusement how I became a "victim" of his
remarkable capacity to remember even minor exchanges. He asked
me about my career plans twice. One exchange was particularly
memorable. I was then a boarding student at the University College
of Addis Ababa. As usual, he visited at dinnertime. He moved about in
the dinning hall, often stopping at tables and randomly chatting with
students. He stopped at our table and fired the expected question at

---

2 Mandela, Nelson. *Long Walk to Freedom*, Little, Brown and Company, USA, 1994, p.255.

us. He turned to me as well and asked, "What are you going to study? What do you want to be?"

"I have not decided yet as to what career I want to pursue. I will soon decide," I said apprehensively.

"How is it possible that you do not have a good idea of what you want to do at this stage of your studies? What year are you?" he asked clearly puzzled, if not unhappy.

"I am about to finish my second year. I will choose soon," I replied rather meekly.

A few others also gave the same response. He was disappointed with our evasive answers that showed indecision. Our answers did not give him what he expected to hear. He wanted to hear about our interests in his priority fields. In my case, his questioning did not end after my answer.

"Did you not give the same answer last time when We asked you about your choice of career?" he asked remembering, to my embarrassment, a reply I indeed gave six months before.

"Yes, I did give the same answer. I am trying to choose a field. It is not easy," I explained uncomfortably.

"There are so many areas that are important to the country. Why should you have a problem choosing?" he rhetorically asked and moved on..

Two decades and a half later, I was again asked to explain why I did not meet an expectation that I should have fulfilled. In 1972, when I was about to report at the United Nations Development Programme, the Minister of Education, Ato Seifu Maheteme Selassie, who was Chairman of the commissions I was responsible for, told me that the Emperor had to give permission. At the Minister's request, I had delayed my departure for a year to direct an education sector study. Respecting his promise that the delay would be no more than a year, he arranged an audience with the Emperor and helpfully requested my release explaining that the experience in an international organization would be good and enriching for future service. We were hoping that the Emperor would not ask for how long, but he did. The Minister indicated that it would be for a short period, perhaps six months.

I was back in Addis Ababa a year later attending a UNDP conference at the conclusion of which the Emperor hosted a reception for the conference participants at the Jubilee Palace. The Chief Aide-de-Camp insisted that, now as a United Nations staff member, I should be presented and pay my respects to the Emperor like the other participants. When the Chairman of the Conference presented me, the Emperor popped up the question I was afraid he could pose, "Weren't you supposed to be back after six months?"

"The United Nations system is a very large organization and offers a lot in terms of experience. A longer experience would be very beneficial," I repeated the argument that the Minister gave when I left for the UNDP and hoping the Emperor would not press the matter further. He did not. I was also relieved that the kind minister who, to help me get a release, had indicated a short duration of my stay at the United Nations, was not there to account why I was exceeding the authorized six-month absence.

This was the last time I saw this great person who had influenced generations and left his mark on the Ethiopia he led so prominently for over half a century. The study of what kind of person the Emperor was, however limited, is just as compelling as the study of his achievements and political role. The attempt in this book thus focuses on Haile Selassie, the person.

Tafari Makonnen, later Haile Selassie I, Emperor of Ethiopia, was born on July 23, 1892 in Ejersa Goro, Harargue, in Eastern Ethiopia. He was the tenth child of Ras Makonnen and Woizero Yeshimebet Abba Deffar; none of the nine children born before Tafari lived beyond early childhood. A story goes that Yeshimebet named her son Tafari (one who is feared) following a dream she had. She claimed that she was told in the dream that she will have a son and he would be named Tafari.[3] Ras Makonnen had an older son, Yilma, who died at the age of

---

3 Belete, Haile Gyorgis, *The History of Ras Makonnen* (from Amharic Translation by Kinfe Gabriel Altaye), Commercial Printing Press, Addis Ababa, 1996 p.42.

thirty-four, only months after he was appointed Governor of Harargue at his father's passing.

As a great grandson of King Sahle Selassie of Shewa and grandnephew of Emperor Menelik, Tafari Makonnen was of royal blood on his father's side. His father, Ras Makonnen, a Shewan, was eight years younger than Atse Menelik. Makonnen's mother was Menelik's aunt. Haile Selassie's mother, Yeshimebet, came from families of 'balabat" and nobles' in Woreilu, Wollo. She had to be from a family with standing to be chosen as a wife to the Ras, a man of royal heritage and with a promising future. She died before Tafari reached the age of two in 1894.

Ras Makonnen did his best to ensure that his son was prepared for a future in which Ethiopia would increase its contacts with Europe. In addition to the traditional schooling, Ras Makonnen ensured his son got skills to communicate and learn from Europeans. He retained a Dr. Vitalien from Guadeloupe, and an Ethiopian Catholic priest, Abba Samuel, to tutor Tafari in French and broaden his knowledge. While this education was limited by contemporary standards, it was then a rarely available schooling.[4]

Makonnen took a daring step in retaining Catholic tutors for his son. Although Tafari was also given the best of the traditional church schooling, the choice of a foreign Catholic tutor to educate his son must have raised eyebrows, and possibly subjected Makonnen to criticism. Such a step could have resulted in a hostile reaction from the powerful and conservative Ethiopian Orthodox Tewahedo Church. In fact, speculation about possible influence on Haile Selassie's faith by the Catholic teachers surfaced from time to time. It is likely that his tolerant and flexible attitude towards other faiths could be a result of this initial exposure.

Makonnen's standing as a devout follower of the Ethiopian Orthodox Tewahedo Church was so well established that his loyalty to the church was not seriously questioned. Besides, Tafari demonstrated

---

4 Haile Selassie I. *My Life and Ethiopia's Progress* 1892-1937. Translation and Annotation by Ullendorf, Edward. Oxford University Press, 1976 p.18-19.

throughout his life his loyalty to the Orthodox Tewahedo faith by going to church regularly, strictly observing fast and church holidays, and materially providing for church activities.[5]

The Emperor paid warm tribute to Abba Samuel, his tutor, when he wrote about his early schooling. He credited this teacher in his autobiography as the source for direction and guidance in his boyhood. The Emperor described Abba Samuel as a humble man of God who, as it is often quoted, "gathered knowledge like a bee."[6] The young Tafari owed his tutors much, for they helped him to be modestly bilingual. More important, they instilled in him respect for education and an interest in what the outside world could offer.

The Emperor cherished the memory of his relationship with his father as "special" and one, which he recalled with emotion, with reverence.[7] They were close, despite the fact the father and son did not live together during the boy's formative years. Makonnen was often away on campaigns. Emperor Menelik sent Ras Makonnen on battle missions to Shewa, Wallamo, and Tigray. For a while, Makonnen was away as governor of Tigray. The short father and son reunions between campaigns and during the times the Ras stayed in his governorate of Harargue made up for the long separations. The father-son relationship became understandably special because of Tafari's mother's death in her early thirties. Still Makonnen's absence forced him to leave his son in the care of friends and trusted guardians, notably Kegnazmatch Haile Selassie and Kegnazmatch Koletch. Though materially well provided, Tafari was deprived in his early years of the daily attention and parental association so important in the life of a child.

Ras Makonnen was among the few of Menelik's officials who were

---

5 A special publication issued by the Ethiopian Orthodox Church in November 2000, entitled His Imperial Majesty Atse Haile Selassie and the Ethiopian Church, in connection with the interment of his remains provides detailed information on his contributions to the Church. Addis Ababa, 2000.

6 Haile Selassie I. *My Life and Ethiopia's Progress* 1892-1937. Translation and Annotation by Ullendorf, Edward. Oxford University Press, 1976 pp18.

7 Ibid, p.19.

exposed to Europe. He traveled to Italy as principal negotiator in efforts to prevent war. He went to England as special envoy to attend the coronation of King Edward VII in 1902. He had also traveled to Jerusalem. The friendship he nurtured and the contacts he had with foreigners locally in Harer, especially with Arthur Ribaud, were also an influence on his interest in European ways and education. Makonnen befriended Rimbaud, the French adventurer, and at times a "gunrunner", during the Frenchman's "bittersweet" visits and stay in Ethiopia in the 1880-1890. Rimbaud was unhappy with Emperor Menelik for refusing to authorize payments to a supplier who Rimbaud was representing.

Makonnen valued his association with Rimbaud, and he kept in touch with him, writing to him when Rimbaud was bedridden seriously ill in France. Rimbaud and other foreigners respected and admired the Ras who, some felt, "could have been more suitably a priest, a scholar, or a philosopher, than a soldier, or a governor."[8] They appreciated Makonnen's studious nature, his strong religious faith, and his belief in education. Haile Selassie's enlightenment, religious tolerance, and his reformist inclination, which were initially considered radical, were likely rooted in these traits and lessons his father passed on.

Makonnen saw in his son's alertness and keen mind a future that he hoped his son would shape with his intellect, rather than with the force of arms. He wisely invested a good deal in Tafari's careful upbringing, education, and early involvement in governance. Makonnen laid the foundation that enabled the young prince to realize his potentials and to cope with the great challenges he faced throughout his life.

An important but often underestimated or even ignored influence that shaped Haile Selassie's life was his own large family of which he was the patriarch. He provided the moral guidance and the support while his children and grandchildren gave him joy and comfort. A strong family man, he was a steady and firm source of inspiration particularly to his grand and great grandchildren. He was known to attach a lot of

---

8 Starkie, Enid, Arthur *Rimbaud*. New Directions Books, 1961, p.390.

importance to "family hour" at home and enjoyed his hours with his young grandchildren. He proudly showed up at public events such as school sports events with some of his youngest grandchildren

However, tragedies plagued him all his life. He "stoically" coped with the many family losses. The tragedies started with the death of his mother when he was only a small child. His father died when he was in his teens. The teacher, Abba Samuel, that he liked so much drowned at a lake now called Haremaya in a boating accident in mid-June, 1915, and Tafari, then a young governor, barely survived the tragic incident.

His daughters, Zenebe Work and Tsehay died prematurely in 1934 and 1942. His second oldest son, Makonnen who was talked about as a contender to succeed the Emperor, died in May 1957 in a car accident.[9] The Empress to whom he was happily married for a half a century and another son, Sahle Selassie died in 1961 and 1962 respectively. The deaths of these and other members of his family, not to mention the loss of close friends and associates, mercilessly punctuated his long life. They occurred at intervals that gave him no respite from mourning. This sad side of his life is often given passing reference, if at all. As the Emperor persevered, despite the hurt of such losses, these ordinarily devastating experiences must have influenced his perceptions and character. They helped him become a self-reliant, realistic, and a tough-minded and God-fearing individual.

But these losses did not end his agony. He learnt a year before his death, while in detention, that his popular grandson, Commander Eskinder Desta, was executed together with fifty-nine of his former senior officials on November 23, 1974. Many of these officials were individuals he had known and mentored; most had started from humble beginnings in status and served their country with dedication. The Emperor's sorrow only ended in 1975 when the military murderers reportedly entered his place of confinement, killed him, and buried him

---

9 Mengesha, Haile Maryam. *Mot Amba Derso Mels* (Return From Death Village), Commercial Printing Press, 2001, pp.118–120.

insensitively in the Palace grounds. His remains were dug out from the ignoble burial on Palace grounds and were interred in the mausoleum in the Trinity Church in Addis Ababa two and half decades later. The EPRDF government in power, while allowing a private service and ceremony, denied him the funeral ceremony and the honor due a head of state. Many African heads of state and world leaders would have participated and honored the man whose eightieth birthday was recognized and honored Africa-wide, as called for by the Organization of African Unity.

2

Claim and Rise to Power

Tafari Makonnen's first appointment to public office was as governor of Gara Mulletta in Harargue Province with the rank of Dejazmatch at thirteen.[10] The appointment was, for all practical purposes nominal, for Tafari was appointed to the post so that he could become a student of government while his experienced guardians did the actual governing. His climb to greater levels of responsibility sped up, and he became Governor of Selale and Sidamo, and then eventually was appointed to govern Harergue. At seventeen he was given this coveted post–one where his father's rule and influence was for years dominant. Empress Taitu, with the approval of the powerful individuals around her, appointed Tafari to his father's post of governor of Harargue on the second round of appointments to this post after Ras Makonnen died. Makonnen's half-brother who was the first to succeed the Ras died only after a few months in office. Dedjazmatch Balcha, who Tafari replaced, followed for a while. Tafari's appointment to the sought after post in Harar was a significant acknowledgement and recognition of his abilities and promising status

Tafari was Regent and Crown Prince for twelve years from 1916 to 1928 when he was crowned Negus. He became Emperor in 1930 and remained so until 1974 when he was overthrown. He ruled as Emperor for

---

10 Belete, Haile Gyorgis. *The History of Ras Makonnen* (from Amharic Translation by Kinfe Gabriel Altaye), Commercial Printing Press, Addis Ababa, August 1996, 2001, p.74.

forty-four years. Including the early internship period, he was in positions of influence and power, albeit in varying degrees, for over six decades.

Divergent versions of Tafari's ascendancy to the imperial throne are told. There are those who contend that he conspired and intrigued to become and even stay as Emperor. Others applaud him as a deserving victor in the struggle for the throne. The latter further stress that, without him, the progressive achievements and the international standing Ethiopia attained in the twentieth century would have taken long in coming.

Some critics even accuse him of foul play in the deaths of both Empress Zawditu to assume power and, later, Ledj Iyasu to stay in power. One story is he expedited Zawditu's death by ordering her servants to bathe her, contrary to her Swedish doctor's advice, with cold water while she was in a state of diabetic shock. She had collapsed on hearing the news of the death of her rebellious husband, Ras Gugsa, at the battle of Qwana on 31 March 1930. However, the same source doubts the veracity of this story in the same page by asserting "the truth about how the Empress died is not known. This made it easy for the rumor-mongers."[11] It is difficult to understand why the news would come as a devastating shock when the Empress had authorized the use of force to put down her husband's revolt. My grandfather, Kegnazmatch Dehne Wolde Maryam, who had served Emperor Menelik and was very close to the Empress, recorded in his diary that the Empress was told of her husband's defeat, but not of his death, because she was seriously ill.[12] He wrote that she died unaware of Gugsa's demise, thus confirming the Emperor's unequivocal assertion that the bad news was kept from her in order not to aggravate her serious health condition.[13]

---

11 Gebru, Dawit. *Kentiba Gebru Desta*, Bole Printing Press Addis Ababa, 1993, p.223.

12 Wolde Maryam, Dehne, *Diary*, Unpublished. 1937-1939 p.52.

13 Haile Selassie I. *My Life and Ethiopia's Progress 1892-1937.* Translation and Annotation by Ullendorf, Edward, Oxford University press, 1976, p.163.

Tafari Makonnen had already neutralized both Iyasu and the Empress. Except at the start of her reign, the Empress was virtually relegated to symbolic existence. The formal division of responsibilities between her and Tafari Makonnen was, in effect, a decision to give him the task of running the government. He had removed her loyalists including Dehne through assignments to provinces or influencing them to join his camp. Dehne was very loyal to the Empress because of his long service to her father, Emperor Menelik. The Empress was also godmother to Dehne's three daughters, a tie that made his loyalty even stronger. He was first denied access to the Empress and then assigned to the then Arussi province. He was accused of association with Dedjazmatch Abba Wukaw Birru who briefly resisted against what he believed to be a Tafari coup underway.

Some suspect that Ledj Iyasu was, in the end, dispensed with to ensure that opponents and the Italians would not use him as a rallying point after the Maychew defeat in 1935. The Italians might have planned to use him as a figurehead to enhance their colonial ambitions.

Ledj Iyasu, a prince considered intelligent and reformist, unfortunately made his own exit from the political scene easy. His indiscretions alienated the conservative and powerful. Even Menelik loyalists, many of whom would have fought for him if he had stayed clear of controversies, did not stand by him. Berihun Kebede in his comprehensive and informative book posits a plausible contention that Tafari was not strong enough to use intrigue to win over to his side or win against the then powerful officials around the throne.[14] He was supported by most of the ecclesiastical and political leaders of the time. Judging from the relative absence of popular uprising or opposition, the choice of Tafari as Regent and Crown Prince was accepted as a measure that served the interest of the country.

Tafari has been described as an astute leader. There were also helpful factors that stood him well in his political pursuit of and hold

---

14 Kebede, Berihun. *The History of Atse Haile Selassie*, Artistic Printing Press, September 28 2000, Addis Ababa, p.39.

to power. He had legitimacy to claim the throne, education, leadership skills, and a progressive outlook a la Menelik. As Makonnen's son and Menelik's distant cousin, he had acceptable credentials of lineage, even though Iyasu and Zawditu were the stronger contenders because of their direct succession birthrights as Menelik's offspring and succeeded to the throne after Menelik's death.

Tafari's father's renown as a war-hero and his father's loyal followers further provided the son an advantageous base to start his ascendancy. The fact that Makonnen had left few personal enemies was helpful. Makonnen's assignments in the provinces kept him, to some extent, far away from the rivalries and intrigues of the court. He was rarely in the capital. His war exploits and good administration of his provinces, especially Harargue, earned him wide respect. Makonnen had hence left Tafari a reservoir of goodwill and a positive heritage of achievement. Both were important in a society where lineage and family background were priority considerations.

Menelik had also given young Tafari fatherly care after Makonnen's death. The Emperor brought young Tafari to his court and made him learn the ways of the court, exposing him to the powerful leaders of the time. In terms of acceptance, Menelik's patronage made Tafari a close member, not just a relative, of the family. Tafari had already been initiated in a leadership role as a young governor of Gara Mulletta area.[15] So, the internship period provided a further and better exposure to new ideas and European technology and thinking. Menelik's curiosity and willingness to embrace new ideas, gadgets, and skills must have inspired and cultivated young Tafari's appetite for progress and innovations.

Tafari Makonnen had, more importantly, the personal attributes that helped him in the attainment and maintenance of power. He had patience and a sense of timing and courage. He saw Iyasu got embroiled in controversies and collided with the church and the overly conservative nobility and was heading for trouble. Tafari did not need

---

15 Belete, Haile Gyorgis. *The History of Ras Makonnen* (from Amharic Translation by Kinfe Gabriel Altaye). Commercial Printing Press, Addis Ababa, 1996, 73-74.

to press the latter's removal too early. With regard to Empress Zawditu, he calculated that he had to wait, for an overzealous effort to push her aside could backfire. He wisely accepted and respected the decision to share power with Empress Zawditu. He took his time in alienating her and gradually eroding her support and power.

Jones and Monroe underscored Tafari's virtues of patience and progressive inclinations when they described his struggle to power. They wrote, "Tafari's ideas were planted in firm bedrock of common sense. He was also infinitely patient." He was pitted against the nobility that 'deplored the newfangled notions which filled' his head.[16] The notions were the European-style changes he advocated in government, particularly the institution of the civil service system and the strengthening of relations with the outside world.

Throughout his life, Tafari also showed remarkable patience and self-control on occasions where others around him were under stress or gloom. For example, he had to cut short his state visit to Brazil in 1960 to cope with an attempted *coup d'état* at home. On the flight back, the members of the entourage were so tense they could not take food and drinks. In contrast, the Emperor reportedly enjoyed his meals with relish and fully relaxed. Even at the time of his deposition or in detention he did not lose his poise and self-control.

Tafari was in the forefront of those who, during Menelik's rule, saw the benefits of change and contacts with Europe. This group has seen that changes have introduced better arms, the railway line, justice, and the start of western-style primary education. However vaguely progress was conceived or defined, Tafari could count on those few who supported progress, or at least were not threatened by it. Even the staunchest supporters of the more conservative Empress saw the advantages the progressive and talented Tafari could bring to the governance of the country. Even partisans such as Dehne saw the arrangement as one that served the best interests of the country and

---

16 Jones, A.B.M. & Monroe, E. *The History of Abyssinia*, Oxford University Press, 1935 Oxford, p.160.

accommodated conflicting demands and pressures.[17]

Exposure to European culture and ways, particularly French, presented him as forward-looking in the eyes of the contending forces and the people. His visits as an emissary to Italy, France, Great Britain, Sweden, and Jerusalem enriched his credentials. He carefully cultivated his international contacts and support with the few local diplomatic representatives and foreign community. They helped with advice and information, and bolstered his image as a progressive leader who had broad interests and vision. When he became Emperor as Haile Selassie I, he was already viewed as a "promising modernizer."

His public relations skills also served him well throughout his public life. He had a congenial and personal approach to foreigners while keeping a measured aloofness. He charmed them in conversations, engaging discussions about the personal sides of their lives. He often gave receptions, memento and souvenirs to mark encounters memorable. Sometimes visitors to the Palace helped themselves and snuck out with mementos, such as teaspoons! One visitor jovially showed me a teaspoon that he had smuggled out after attending a tea reception at the Jubilee Palace. Such unauthorized souvenir collection was known to the palace staff.

The animals in the zoo on the grounds of the well-kept Jubilee Palace also made lasting impressions on dignitaries and nationals alike. Attorney General Robert Kennedy visited Ethiopia in the early sixties. In conjunction with his visit, the Prize Trust had organized, a public lecture where he was the guest speaker. Because of this hosting role, I accompanied him to the Jubilee Palace where he had a private audience with the Emperor. We were exiting the Palace when he was treated with an unexpected encounter. He found himself inches away from two cheetahs that had been brought to the Palace door. This was the last place he expected to run into cheetahs. It was the reassuring words of the minister seeing him off that allayed his instinctive hesitation and

---

17 Wolde Maryam, Dehne, *Diary*, Unpublished, 1937-1939. p.50.

gave him the confidence to pat them and enjoy their beauty.

Not long before President John Kennedy's death, the Emperor visited the United Sates. He very much appreciated the warm hospitality extended to him then by the President and large and admiring crowds, including the famous New York tickertape parade. When President Kennedy died, the Emperor, given his age and disposition, could have sent an envoy to the funeral rather than go through the travel stress and the trying march in the funeral procession and the elaborate ceremony. His attendance at the funeral was yet another example of a personal gesture that played well to a foreign community, in this case among the Kennedy family and the American public. Kennedy's death had also a personal meaning to the Emperor who only six years before Kennedy's death had, due to a car accident, lost a comparably young son – Prince Makonnen in 1957. President Kennedy was killed in 1963 at the age of forty-five.

The Emperor gave audience and extended hospitality to conference participants, philanthropists, and individual visitors to the country provided a responsible institution or official initiated the request for audience. At the personal level, he often struck up conversations and made his visitors comfortable. I once took with me a British surveyor who had done a study for the Prize Trust to explain the technical aspects of the exercise to the Emperor. I introduced the expert stressing that he had completed his work despite recent heart attacks and need for an extended rest. The Emperor ignored the study for the most part of the meeting and told the man that he should not have been working so soon after his release from the hospital.

"You are not a young man. You should first be healthy and take care of your health," he counseled the expert.

"I have to work. I cannot be idle. Whatever will happen will happen, Your Majesty," the expert insisted.

"No, that is not right. You must take care of your health first. You must," the Emperor responded with concern. Very touched by the personal interest the Emperor showed, the expert talked about the incident and the personal concern and interest the Emperor has shown whenever he got the opportunity.

Timing, heritage, political skills, courage and determination strengthened the Emperor's claim and rise to power and sustained him in the decades of his leadership. These attributes enabled him to become "the larger-than life personality." No less a factor was, as Ehrlich Haggai puts it, "the capacity of the Ethiopian society for allowing born leaders to move into leadership positions."[18]

---

18 Ehrlich Hagai. *Ethiopia and the Challenge of Independence.* Boulder, Colorado: Lynne Reiner Publishers Inc, 1986, p.6.

3

The Education Emperor

When Emperor Haile Selassie entered the Ethiopian scene, the need for a modern or a western educational program in Ethiopia was felt only among a handful of influential persons, led by Emperor Menelik. Haile Selassie gave priority to education and started taking action soon after he came into power. He pushed for the expansion of education increasing the national enrollment to 5000 and the schools to 30 before the Ethio-Italian war. He lived to see the enrollment of a few thousand grow in 1970-1971 to 795.000 students, enrolled in 1530 government and 1304 non-government schools. Five thousand of those students attended post-secondary institutions.[19] In light of the poor state of education when he began, the constraints of resources, absence of local teachers, and other challenges he faced, these figures reflect significant achievement.

Even more important, he provided leadership that infused in his government and among the people the sense that education was the foundation for development and for each individual's success. He was convinced that "education is a proven medicine." Such a conviction was no surprise. The importance of education, especially the value of Western education, has been inculcated in him in his youth, and he himself had reaped the fruits of his own limited schooling.

19 The Report of The Education Sector Review. *Education: Challenge To The Nation, Addis Ababa*, 1972, EXHIBIT II-B-1, p, II-5 –II-7.

The Emperor and his colleagues promoted quality education made available to students selected on the basis of high academic standards. Respected colleges and universities abroad recognized this fact and they granted admission and assistance to the graduates of the Ethiopian colleges. Those who studied abroad returned to the country on completion of their studies, despite the allures of comfort and economic betterment. They returned to constitute a small but significant trained manpower, further attesting to the achievements of the Emperor's leadership.

The Emperor understood education as an investment in the future, and, as such, he made it of the highest priority. He was convinced, and rightly so, that those who had the opportunity for education, especially those with specific skills, would determine the country's destiny. Education was the means for national unity and the key to development. He deemed its promotion as his special, lifelong responsibility. The Emperor remained "possessive" of the education sector, directly involving himself and keeping the ministerial portfolio for himself until expansion of the educational system forced him to delegate responsibilities.

What was most telling about his committment was his personal involvement and participation in activities and the incentives he employed to encourage education.

The Emperor's interest was enduring, and he made available significant resources of his own as well towards the realization of his commitment. In addition to starting one of the most productive public schools, Tafari Makonnen School on April 27, 1925 when he was crown prince, the Emperor gave his former palace to the national university, and launched humanitarian activities that addressed needs of the physically challenged.

His interest was not confined to Ethiopia. At the Emperor's instigation, Ethiopia offered one hundred scholarships to students from other African countries for study at the then Haile Selassie I University. I recall the great interest and the high volume of applications from throughout the continent that we received at the Registrar's Office where I was at the time Associate Registrar. The program proved to be enriching because it exposed Ethiopian students to other Africans and the freedom struggles in the continent.

The few following stories illustrate his sustained and pervasive personal involvement in and commitment to the promotion of education.

Christmas Gifts and Prizes

Like thousands of others, the first exposure to the Emperor was for most of us at Christmas. For many years in post-war Ethiopia, all the students in the capital went to the Palace or to Janhoy Meda to receive Christmas gifts handed out by the Emperor and the senior members of the royal family. The gift for each student consisted of a sweater with distinctive colors assigned to schools, a raisin cake, and an orange. Students as well as parents who enjoyed hearing about their children's experiences awaited with anticipation this popular annual event. The Emperor attached so much importance to this annual gesture that he once thoughtfully brought us at college clothing material from abroad, where he was traveling during a Christmas season. Each student was given material for a suit. As the years went by, the size of the student population made it impossible for the Emperor to continue his popular Christmas gift giving.

The Emperor also visited school campuses and boarding facilities periodically. These visits were special occasions for us because he conversed with us about our career plans, our studies and so forth. The fruit he brought for boarding students were also a rare treat. At the end of supper, in his presence, we were served oranges, banana, and grapes. He sometimes gave advice on the usefulness of eating fruits and vegetables. Those of us who never had apples, almost all of us, were given lessons by the "Shime," the Old Man, as he was affectionately called, about the benefits of eating them with the peels. Of course, sometimes students took advantage of these visits and complained about the quality of the food in the boarding facilities.

In the early years, the top three students in each class in the final annual examinations in the schools in the capital went to the Palace to receive prizes, books and certificates from the Emperor. This practice, which went on for many years, also stopped when the student population growth made it unmanageable.

Those who successfully completed undergraduate college programs were virtually assured of graduate education abroad, with all expenses paid by government or donor assistance. As students left for study abroad, and as they returned, the Emperor found time to meet them; he impressed upon them that the country expected dedicated service especially from those who, at great cost, studied abroad. Prince Beide Mariam Makonnen, a grandson of the Emperor, cited in his eulogy at the Emperor's memorial service a very telling example of how the Emperor felt on this subject. The Prince quoted the Emperor's reply to a letter from one of his grandsons. The Emperor told the young man that he was happy to receive his letter then, in no uncertain terms, told the young man that he, and his parents, would be much happier, only truly happy, if and when he completes his studies and returned to serve his country.

The fatherly pampering of the school population continued for years. Young people perceived him as a guardian who had interest in their welfare. The Emperor had established such a rapport that when, in one instance in the late forties, the student body in the Tafari Makonnen school went on strike against the school administration, students refused to air their grievances to anybody else but him. The complaints were mixed and the causes were festering for quite a while.

The students claimed the Canadian Jesuit teachers were oppressive and very much biased in favor of Catholic students. A few students were even subjected to mob beating by their striking schoolmates who, based on information of doubtful merit, accused them of informing on the student body. Meetings were held in classrooms and even in a churchyard where pledges were made to stand together. Student

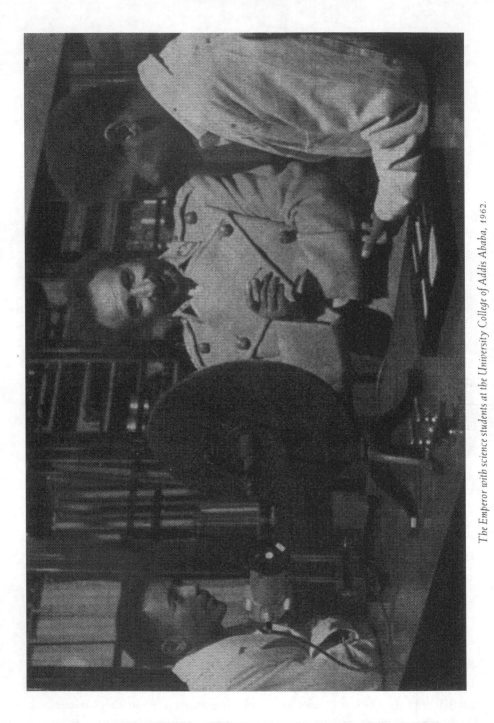

The Emperor with science students at the University College of Addis Ababa, 1962.

leaders exhorted the student body. Professor Mesfin Wolde-Mariam, the well-known academic, then a student, exhorted the crowd to be courageous in the tradition of their forefathers. He spiced up his speech by reminding the assembly that, during the Italo-Ethiopian war, "Ethiopian women folk, in the absence of other means, threw their *mamasaya* or stirring rod for cooking to try to down Italian bombing aircraft." He did not at the time provide figures as to how many planes were downed by the *mamasaya* missiles!

This student strike was probably the first serious one in post Ethiopian–Italian war. It was, however, preceded by one before the war that resulted in some of the strike leaders being sent abroad for studies as punishment. The Emperor, then Crown Prince Tafari, was reportedly the one who at the time recommended that the strike leaders be sent abroad for studies instead of being whipped and expelled from school. Nearly all returned to serve their country under the Emperor.

In the Tafari Makonnen School strike, the Emperor was forced to come to the school and hear our complaints. Officials including the Emperor's Chief Aide-de-Camp who had come earlier to persuade us to change our minds and take our petition were rebuffed. We wanted the Emperor to hear our complaints directly.

About four o'clock on the strike day, Imperial Bodyguard soldiers cordoned off the school and took positions in the school grounds. The Emperor came at suppertime, obviously unhappy that we had insisted on his coming and snubbed his officials. The grievances were read by one of the senior students. The Emperor criticized us, saying that, instead of striking, we should have presented our grievances to him during one of his many visits. He also stressed that some students who had access to the Palace could have conveyed our messages to him and indicated our grievances would be looked into. A few months later, the decision came. Though thirty-seven of us who were identified by the school officials as strike leaders were transferred to other schools, he found it important and had come to hear our grievances. We had our day in court.

Engineer Demissie Abebe, told me three stories that showed the Emperor's constant interest and commitment to the educational effort. They are presented under the titles: *The Sidamo Eight Go Imperial, The Little River Girl, and The Skinny Boy Flexes His Muscles.*

The Sidamo Eight Go Imperial

Demissie's parents, as was the case with the other Amhara families that had migrated to Sidamo with the advent of liberation, were interested in teaching their children Amharic in the church schools. After learning to read and write at home, Demissie and his brother joined the Saint Michael Church School.

Luckily for the children in the area, the government broke new ground by establishing a public school in Yirgalem, under the leadership of an able educational administrator, Ato Bogale Walelu. This gentleman had to work hard to get the school going. He had to visit families in their homes to convince parents to send their children to the public school. He visited Demissie's home several times to convince his parents to enroll their two sons in the public school. Their reluctance was, in part, due to their unfounded fear that the school will convert their sons, predominantly Orthodox Tewahedo Christians, to other faiths. Administrator Bogale concentrated on the well-known and respected families in the community in his recruitment drive. If he could win the community leaders over and get them to send their children to the public school, he was confident the rest of the community would follow. Eventually, thanks to this committed and persevering educator, many joined the public school.

Demissie was still in the fourth grade when the Emperor visited Sidamo in the mid–forties. One of his important stops was the public school where he spent time talking to the students and assessing their educational progress. After the visit, the Emperor asked Bogale to identify four students for him to take to Addis Ababa and, potentially, send them for study abroad. The administrator selected the best eight, strictly on merit with advice from other teachers. Demissie was one of the students consulted and selected. The Emperor took no part in the selection and gave no criteria except that they should be the best available. The Emperor knew neither the students nor their parents. The administrator presented to the Emperor eight students ostensibly to enable the Emperor to choose four. The ingenious administrator instinctively felt that the Emperor would not turn down any of the eight if he could show that they were all good choices. His instincts proved right. After talking to the students individually, the Emperor decided to take all eight. These chosen few were brought to the Emperor's temporary camp and housed in a tent. Two brothers from Borena were later added to the group, reportedly at the request of parents.

The reluctance of parents to let their children go so far away was somewhat minimized when they were assured that the young people would be under the patronage of the Emperor. The students travelled by lorry sitting on top of food provisions as part of the royal entourage during the return to the capital. As the Emperor stopped at villages and towns such as Shashemene and Debre Zeyt for official visits, tents were quickly put up for the boys. They were free to visit the small village-towns where they stopped and moved in and out of the temporary imperial camp without questions. In Addis Ababa, they were accommodated in the palace grounds for about twenty days until they joined a boarding school, attracting attention as the Emperor's special boys.

The Emperor instructed the Ministry of Education to have the students admitted at the favored "Kotebe" school, officially Haile Selassie Secondary School. The Ministry authorities, probably because of space shortage and the qualifications of the young students, instead enrolled them in Tafari Makonnen School. The Sidamo Eight left the Palace provided with items ranging from mattress to shorts.

The Ministry only accepted the students to comply with the instructions of the Emperor. The new arrivals had to sleep for a while in a storeroom until accommodations were arranged. A month after their enrollment at Tafari Makonnen School, the students who had expected to attend the school at Kotebe, realized that they were enrolled in the wrong school. Angered by what they thought was deceit in enrolling them in a different school, the eight went to the Palace to see the Emperor, who readily received them. Abba Hanna, the man designated to serve as liaison with the eight, arranged the audience for them. The Emperor explained the placement problem as briefed and assured them things would work out. Softened by the imperial explanation, they continued at the Tafari Makonnen School. The Sidamo Eight group produced two engineers, a lawyer, a medical doctor, and a teacher who served their country with distinction.

Abdullah A. Abogne (Abdosh) also describes in detail how he and fourteen other Moslem students from different provinces were, like the Sidamo Eight, imperial "guests of honor" for a month in recognition of excellent academic work. To top it all, they were given full scholarships to pursue secondary and higher education in the capital.[20]

A Little Girl Meets the Emperor

The case of a little girl who the Emperor adopted during the same Sidamo visit sounds like a fairy tale. On his way back to the capital, the Emperor had stopped by a river in a rural community. The small river provided water for residents of the area. The Emperor and his entourage had walked to the river where they found several women washing clothes. The Emperor saw a little girl playing near her mother, who was busy scrubbing her laundry.

The Emperor beckoned the little girl to come to him. Not intimidated by the entourage and the invitation from a total stranger, she readily approached him. She got hold of the edge of his cape and looked up at him as if she had known him for a long time.

The mother stood astonished at her daughter's uninhibited cozying up with the "king." The Emperor was also pleasantly surprised by the

20 Abogne (Abdosh), Abdullah A. *Bercha: Cryptic Tales of Harar & Glimpses of My Life*, Addis Ababa, Artistic Printing Enterprise, 2003, p.191.

girl's friendliness.

"What is her name? Why don't you give her to Us? We will raise and educate her. You can visit her any time you wish," he earnestly asked the mother. He was even more surprised by the unhesitating response of the mother.

"Nothing will make me happier than seeing my child raised by 'Janhoy,' she quickly replied putting the interest of the girl before her own motherly instinct not to part with her child.

"Give the mother a pass so that she can come and visit whenever she wants. Take the child to the Empress," he instructed. He raised the child and later sent her abroad for education. There were others whom he took under his wings and educated.

One could cite many revealing incidents about the critical influence the Emperor routinely exerted in the education process. Sometimes, he intervened in seemingly minor cases, yet his interventions often became determining factors for overcoming the prevailing slow and cumbersome bureaucracy and the ever-present financial constraints. School officials, nationals or foreign, recognized and capitalized on the significance of his interventions and involved him to their advantage. How the ingenious Canadian headmaster, Dr.Lucien Matte, of the Tafari Makonnen School resolved his problem with the Ministry of Education and Fine Arts is illustrative.

The Skinny Boy Flexes His Muscles

The Ministry had turned down a request for finance by the headmaster for the installation of gymnastics equipment in the school grounds. Despite Matte's repeated efforts, the Ministry refused to provide the resources. The Emperor was on one of his frequent visits to the School when the headmaster pushed for his request.

During the tour of the dinning hall where the boarding students were having supper, the headmaster deliberately steered the Emperor to a rather skinny young boy who wore a short-sleeve soccer uniform.

He asked the boy to raise his arm and flex his upper arm and show his muscles. The boy did not have much to show. On the contrary, he was a good example of the many young boys who needed to develop their physique. The wily headmaster pursued his case, as he has done so many times, mixing evidence and calculated show of anguish and desperation.

"Your Majesty, I had requested finance to build gymnastics facilities so that boys like this one could become strong and well-developed. Please note how this boy lacks strong muscles. He is physically underdeveloped. I had asked the Ministry of Education and Fine Arts to provide money to buy and install equipment for use by the students. The Ministry did not approve my urgent pleas, contending that it was short of funds. I do not know what to do, Your Majesty."

"I understand your predicament," the Emperor sympathized, no doubt appreciating the headmaster's clever solicitation. The Emperor instructed his aide-de-camp to inform the Ministry that the facilities be installed as a priority. They were put in place forthwith.

This episode had a sequel worth noting. About forty years later, Demissie Abebe who had witnessed the ploy of the skinny boy flexing his muscles saved the same facilities from demolition. A road construction crew was working in the school grounds and the facilities were in the way and targeted for removal. Demissie was the supervising engineer for the construction work. He recalled the difficulties encountered in getting them and he convinced his colleague, the Chief Engineer, to bypass them and leave alone the still intact facilities. They were left in place and were of service for many more years.

The Emperor played a catalytic role to encourage educational initiatives, no matter how small. The students at the Haile Selassie Secondary School launched a small effort to teach children, primarily literacy, in the surrounding farming area. With no money to buy material for their project, they put up a small one-room structure using stones gathered from the area. Branches of trees served as roof. Because it was located on the roadside, the odd structure was easily noticeable.

The Emperor could not but notice it as he drove by on his way to the secondary school and he asked about the structure and its purpose. When he was told students built it as a classroom to teach the children in that rural area, he immediately instructed that a proper school building be built. That school expanded to become a large public school that is still operating.

Initial Hurdles to the Introduction of Education

There were many hurdles to the introduction, much less the expansion of, what was referred to as modern, more correctly western education. The lack of teachers for the newly opened schools necessitated the complex task of getting foreign teachers – first Egyptians, followed by the British, Indian, Canadians and other nationalities. The severe lack of resources in general made the challenge even more formidable. Early in the post-war years, a sliding scale for fees for boarding students was in effect for a while. The higher fees were for children of the royal family and sons of other wealthy families. A lower fee scale was for the children of the merchants and middle-level civil servants who were deemed able to pay. This paying group was a negligible percentage of the boarding population. Even this payment scale was eventually abandoned and education including study abroad for successful students was free for most of Haile Selassie's watch.

Another formidable and initial challenge was the resistance of parents to enroll their children in the few available schools, especially in the rural areas. Farmers wanted their children to tend to their livestock and help on the farms. In some families such as those widowed, the teenage boys and girls supported the whole family. Some families in rural communities still keep children out of school at peak harvest time when extra help is crucial.

A trick perpetrated in Bale Province is illustrative of the complexity and degree of resistance by families. The story was told by one of the young men who unwittingly, but luckily for him, was involved in a hoax that community leaders played on the Emperor. While the Emperor was visiting the region, he pressured the chiefs in the community to give him their sons to take to the schools in the capital. The chiefs did not want to do so but had to somehow comply with the request. Unknown to the Emperor and his party, they picked a number of young boys from the community and presented them to the Emperor as their sons, while hiding their own children. Not suspecting the deception, the Emperor took the substitute boys and enrolled them in schools in the capital. The young man, who told the story was one of those substituted, went abroad on a scholarship. No doubt the door to a new life was opened to the others as well.

Moslem students who pioneered and joined the new schools had their share of problems. They were initially looked at unfavorably due to their community's fears that they may convert to Christianity or be affected by the "decadent Amhara influence."[21]

The Emperor was convinced that the best way to break parents' resistance to sending their children to the new government schools was to convince, first, the *balabbat* and community leaders to send their children to school. They had to set the example. Whenever he went on visits or when such leaders came to the capital, he pressured them to educate their children. He urged provincial governors and educational administrators to keep the pressure on and recruit students. A school established, popularly known as '*balabbat*' or chief school (officially Medhane Alem) at Gulele, west of Addis Ababa, gave priority to the enrollment of young students who came from the provinces. These pioneers went far in their education and served their country in a wide range of professions.

Let Them Go East Too

A former official and educator who directed a division responsible for the management of scholarships granted to Ethiopia by foreign

---

21 Abogne (Abdosh), Abdullah A. *Bercha: Cryptic Tales of Harar & Glimpses of My Life*, Addis Ababa, Artistic Printing Enterprise, 2003, p.192.

governments shared with me an interesting experience. At the time, Ethiopia relied heavily on United Kingdom, France and the United States for help to send able young people for study abroad. These countries were generous in their help, and, understandably, the majority of recipients went to their institutions for study. It was, however, government policy, no doubt partly because of donor pressure, not to send Ethiopians to the socialist countries, even though full diplomatic relations existed with several of them.

The socialist countries, especially the Soviet Union, made many scholarship offers. The director and colleagues saw this as another great opportunity for more young people to get education abroad. They felt that there were scientific and technical areas in which Ethiopian students could be trained in these countries. Aware that this was a sensitive area, the officials decided to get the blessing of the Emperor. His answer came quick and clear. Without advice from anybody, he instructed that such offers be accepted and students go and pursue studies in the sciences and technology. His firm instruction was "let the young go and learn." He opted for this decision fully knowing that the young people could return with ideas that could pose risks for him and his rule. He also knew that his decision would not be to the liking of the donors from the non-socialist countries.

Royal Attention for the Girls

The Emperor encouraged efforts to increase the girl population in the school system in general and provided fatherly care and attention to those few in the high schools and higher institutions. He urged the girls in the high schools in the provinces to continue their studies in college promising them that he will substitute for their parents when they moved to the capital. His often-repeated pledge was:

"You must go on with further studies. You do not have to worry about anything when you come to Addis Ababa. We will take care of and provide you with all your needs. We will be like your parents. God bless you. You have been strong and persevering."

He closely watched their progress during their years in the University College of Addis Ababa. He routinely looked for them whenever he visited the College and asked them about their welfare. In the case of one student, he even went as far as getting her an exemption from attending French language classes in college. She had complained to him that she did not take French in high school since, unlike the case of her classmates, it was not offered in her school. The Emperor imposed on the college president to exempt her from taking the language course.

A Guest for All Occasions

Whether at sporting events, laying the foundation for buildings, and inaugurating a school, the Emperor participated and played catalytic roles by his presence and patronage. He rarely missed presiding over the annual college graduation ceremonies. He handed the diplomas personally to each graduate for many years, thus according special flavor and prestige to these ceremonies. He encouraged the best students and awarded trophies and prizes. Hailu Gebre Hiwot cherished a watch the Emperor gave him for being selected as an all-around student and still nostalgically recalls the Emperor's advice that came with it. He told him not to "let education negatively change your good conduct and qualities that have been recognized to-day."

Many interesting incidents took place on these occasions. Young graduating students received degrees, prizes and gifts from the Emperor who asked questions or commended them as individuals. Some were on the receiving end of his displeasure. One student, who had at a much earlier occasion done something that was considered unacceptable to the Emperor, was to receive his diploma from the Emperor, like all the others. However, it was decided that he would not receive the diploma from the Emperor and that his name would not be called. When the faculty members heard of this intention, they refused to participate in the graduation ceremony, thus creating an embarrassing crisis. A compromise was reached. The student's name was called and he proceeded to receive his diploma from the Emperor who neither handed the diploma nor said anything to the student. The latter went back to his seat equally unflustered. He collected his diploma later. He officially graduated while the Emperor did not recognize him. Nor did the Emperor override the principled objection of the faculty.

The interactions with students took place in a family context. We perceived him almost as a parent and he perceived himself as our guardian. The respect we showed him was in this spirit and as one shown to the elderly or parents, naturally flavored by the imperial aura and reverence. Whatever failures and problems still prevailed in education, no other Ethiopian leader has been so personally committed and achieved so much with so little as Emperor Haile Selassie. He was the Education Emperor.

4

A Prized Experience

My service in the Haile Selassie I Prize Trust was a truly prized experience, for I had a rare opportunity, however briefly, to come in direct contact with one of Ethiopia's most influential leaders. Most of these meetings or audiences dealt with matters related to the estates given to the Trust. In fewer cases, the meetings dealt with issues pertaining to the awards that the Trust gave annually. Although the Trust enjoyed the Emperor's special attention, the organization was not immune to the pressures and machinations with regards to properties.

Though the resolution of the property disputes was essential, they were an utter nuisance and a waste of time, especially of the Emperor's time. He had to be involved because the issues concerned personal property he gave to individuals, as in the case of the Trust. Although many of the disputes dealt with his foundation and involved tension with his close associates and influential personalities, he listened to both sides and fairly settled the disputes. During the hearings, the Trust was almost always on the defensive because claimants often made sure the Emperor was aware of their claims in advance. Often, I was called without any foreknowledge of the subjects for discussion much less of the claims.

The Early Days of the Prize Trust

The Prize Trust was a chartered non-profit organization that sought to recognize excellence in performance in the arts, Ethiopian and African studies, industry, Amharic literature, agriculture, and humanitarian activities. The Trust also gave fellowships and scholarships for specialization and academic achievement. At its establishment, the Emperor gave three farms at Tibila in Arussi, Erer Gota and Hurso in Harargue and some company shares in what was then known the Societe Ethiopia Hôtelière. These were to be the sources, more accurately, potential sources of income for the Trust's activities. With the exception of Erer Gota, which yielded some 30,000 *birr*, about 15,000 US dollars at the time, annual income, the other properties were operating at a loss. Even this small income from Erer Gota, a farm passed on to the Emperor by his father, was realized at the price of much needed improvement of the estate. The farm was deteriorating and the fruit trees aging.

The first business audience I had with the Emperor as the Director of the Trust dealt with the new organization's financing. Unsure of how I was to present myself and how to respond in a first official audience with the one man in Ethiopia whose name caused either awe and respect, or fear and hostility, I felt nervous and intimidated. The guards at the checkpoints in the Menelik Palace grounds, the zealous and officious air of the junior aides I met while making my way to the Emperor's office, and the presence of many senior people milling around all combined to make me feel a mixture of anticipation, uncertainty, and awe.

As soon as I told the guards at the first checkpoint that I had been called to see His Majesty, I was immediately cleared to proceed and offered a salute. Deference was automatically shown to those whose

---

*   The Trustees at the establishment of the Trust: Prime Minister Aklilu Habte Wold, Ato Yilma Deressa, Commander Eskinder Desta,

Ledj Kassa Wolde Maryam, and Ato Yewand-Wossen Mangasha

The Emperor at the opening of the Haile Selassie I Prize with the Director, Dr. Abebe Ambatchew.

presence was summoned by the Emperor. The next officer who cleared my advance to the office was also aware that I was expected. In the final stage before the audience with the Emperor, a courteous aide guided me to the rather poorly lit outer room next to the Emperor's office, where about half a dozen senior government officials stood around chatting in low tones—a couple of governors and top civil servants waiting to see the Emperor. A quick look at the group left no doubt in my mind that I was clearly out of my league. Their inquisitive looks suggested that they were wondering who I was, yet all of them politely acknowledged my greetings.

Abebe Kebede had promised that he would be there to help. He was most involved in the initial conception of the Trust and he was a member of the Trust's Board. More importantly, he has dealt with the Emperor for years as head of the Haile Selassie I Foundation. I needed all the help possible for the item for discussion was no simple matter. It would not be an easy task to inform the Emperor that the properties he donated for the Trust, although potentially significant, could not even cover minimal operating costs of our office.

Fortunately, Abebe walked in only minutes before I was asked to see the Emperor. The deputy aide-de-camp led us into the office where the Emperor was standing in front of his desk. We bowed respectfully and, as we did, the aide-de-camp said good morning obviously on behalf of the Emperor. That was the practice, but the Emperor did not leave us with the proxy greeting. He rather warmly and with a faint smile said good morning. He wore his tan Marshall's uniform, his cape neatly rolling down his shoulders. As it was always the case, he was dressed immaculately with the ties, the suit, and shoes matching appropriately. Next to him stood a senior official from his Secretariat with a notebook and pen in hand to take notes and instructions. Soon after we entered, he signaled with a quick nod that I state my business. The rather attentive and business-like start put me at ease.

The Emperor listened to my brief presentation and Abebe's supportive comments with surprise. He was aware that the Trust would require further allocation, but he did not expect to hear that the Trust had cash to meet operating costs only for a month or two and the properties would not yield significant resources. He paused for a while clearly realizing that what he had been told was not so dire situation. He then instructed his treasurer to give to the Trust a one-time amount of 30000 *birr* and instructed me to submit a detailed budget for his consideration.

Thus, I submitted a budget for an annual allocation of 400,000 *birr* for the awards, operational expenses, and for the development of the properties. It was clear that the Emperor did not foresee such a high level of support in addition to the gifts he already made, but he authorized the requested amount, without which we could not have functioned, from incomes of the Saint George Brewery. The Brewery belonged to him. His speedy approval of the requested budget strongly confirmed that he was serious about the Trust and wanted it to succeed.

The allocation was to be provided after the Brewery had taken care of its taxes, provided for reserve and for its improvement. The annual allocation could hence be less than 400,000 if incomes of the factory fell short after providing for these obligations. If the income exceeded this amount, three quarters of the balance would be the Emperor's while the remaining quarter would be given to the Haile Selassie I Foundation. Apart from these provisions, the document explicitly stated that during his lifetime, "the total ownership of the factory is ours." There was also a provision that indicated that the Brewery assets would be divided equally between the Prize Trust and the Haile Selassie I Foundation after his death.[22] This was amended in a letter dated June 29, 1972 ref 3737/65 from the Ministry of Pen to the General Manager of Saint George Brewery and copied to the Chairman of the Board of Trustees giving the Brewery in total to the Prize Trust. All shares owned by the Brewery were also given to the Trust in a letter dated the same ref: 3738.[23] Both letters instruct the General manager of the Brewery to transfer the said properties to the Trust.

---

22 Instruction issued from the Jubilee Palace with the Emperor's seal dated May 1965.

23 Letters from the Ministry of Pen to the General Manager of the Brewery on June 29, 1972.

Benefactors who establish foundations do so to leave something to be remembered by, to render service, or help a cause. This was what the Emperor also envisaged. In distorted propaganda against the Emperor, the Dergue tried to undermine the motives of the Emperor by contending that he established the Trust for fame and publicity only. The military regime further publicized that the Emperor had illegally acquired the Saint George Brewery and squandered its income, accusing the Emperor of giving the Brewery to the Haile Selassie Foundation and the Prize Trust while continuing to take the income.[24] The Dergue even went as far as belittling the outstanding award recipients as undeserving. The fifty-two meritorious writers, researchers, entrepreneurs, personalities, and institutions can only be undeserving in the minds of people who do not appreciative what the recipients achieved, often over lifetimes of hard work. Detailed information on recipients is found in Berihun Kebede's The History of Atse Haile Selassie[25]

The accusation that the Emperor took for himself the brewery, a public property, is refuted by documentary evidence and the testimony of Ato Bekele Beshah, the person who served as the Brewery's General Manager from the start and who had been involved in the purchase of the factory from two Austrian individuals, George and Manfred Mautner Markhof. Ato Makonnen Habte Wold, Ato Teferra Work Kidane Wold and Ato Bekele Beshah represented the Emperor in reaching an agreement on the purchase on December 22, 1952.[26] Ato Bekele, in an interview in October 2000, confirmed to me categorically that the Emperor borrowed, at his suggestion, the money to buy the then modest Brewery for 500000 birr. The bank where the letter of credit in favor of the sellers was opened in was the Banque de

---

24 Addis Zemen. Pagume 1, 1974.

25 Kebede, Berihun, The History of Atse Haile Selassie, Artistic Printing Press, Addis Ababa, September 2001, pp.529-581.

26 Proces Verbale of Meeting held in Addis Ababa, December 22, 1952.

l'Indochine at Addis Ababa.[27] The Dergue propaganda conveniently avoided mention of the fact that the Emperor bought the Brewery with borrowed money. As regards the yearly allocation to the Prize Trust, it was regularly received, utilized by the Trust, and the accounts audited by Price Waterhouse.

My first impression of the Emperor went unchanged throughout subsequent audiences. In contrast to the elaborate protocol demands that one experienced before entering his office, the atmosphere in his office was serious but not intimidating. The office was brightly lit and spacious, yet not unduly imposing and ostentatious. The same held true in his smaller office at the Jubilee Palace, which was also his residence. The Emperor got to business quickly and his questions were direct and often intended to elicit explanations and views. He listened attentively and conveyed his decision right away or indicated the manner of follow-up.

The Emperor showed very keen and supportive interest in the work of the Trust and its progress. He repeatedly stressed that he expected it to evolve into a respected institution. In one instance, I was summoned to see him following a graduation ceremony in the national university. He noticed me in the audience and, when the ceremony was over and I was about to leave for my office, I heard over the loudspeaker that I was to proceed immediately to the university president's office. An aide took me to the Emperor who was walking back and forth on his old veranda, as he used to do before he gave his Palace to the University. He wanted to impress upon me that the awards, especially the international award named after the Empress, should be given to the truly deserving. He stressed that he attached the highest importance to this award. I assured him this would be the case.

The Emperor encouraged, though not successfully, family and officials to contribute to the Trust, regardless of type or magnitude of donations. The plan for a small library in the Trust was a case in point. He

---

27 Minutes of Meeting between the Emperor's representatives and the sellers, Addis Ababa, December 22, 1952, p.2.

pledged his support and urged others to donate at the inauguration of the offices of the Prize Trust. The Emperor and members of his family, the Trustees, other officials were attending the small but formal ceremony. The Emperor was being shown around the small office building when he came to the combination of library and conference room. In a deliberately raised voice so that those present would hear, he asked me if any of those present had donated books to the library.

"We have established the Trust to encourage and recognize citizens and institutions that have achieved outstanding results. How have others helped the Trust? Have any from among those present here given, for instance, books for the library?" he asked.

The reactions were almost comical. There was a chorus of "we will help!" One earnestly pointed out that he was not asked. A royal highness asked me for a list of the required books making sure that the Emperor heard the request. At the end of the ceremony, the Royal Highness said in a low voice, "don't make the list too long!" Still another, a minister, who was a guest speaker at one of our functions, told the Emperor "I was the first to give a lecture in the Trust. The Director will confirm it." His contribution was, to say the least, different from what the Emperor was suggesting. All these reactions were to assure the Emperor that they supported his establishment of the Trust and were eager to help. The assurances to donate did not, to our chagrin, translate into any follow-up donations, not even into further queries.

No Veto on Award Nominees

What I found admirable and interesting was that the Emperor did not express reservation about, as far as the Trust was concerned, the ceremonial role he was given by the Charter of the Trust. The provisions of the Charter implied that the Emperor only gave the awards, but he did not approve or veto recommendations of the Trustees and the selection committees. This could not have been an easy stance for him, since the Trust was established with his donations and he was used to giving medals and awards to those he approved. The Emperor could have insisted on having the final say on all selections for the awards. This approach and the procedures adopted required tactful explaining to convince him of the absolute necessity that the Trust was, in reality and in public perception, an independent entity. This did not mean that any justifiable reservation of his, with regard to a specific recommendation, did not carry weight. But, if the various levels of the selection committees find his reservation unjustified, we expected him to go along with the recommended candidate. He saw the validity of the approach and complied, despite his expressed misgivings about some of the candidates selected.

Selection committee members consisted of people from the national university, the civil service, and individuals known for their competence, integrity, and objectivity. The selection bodies had a three-tiered committee structure. There were selection sub-committees for each award. A larger body comprising all the members of the selection committees then reviewed the recommendation of each sub-committee. The Director was an ex-officio member who ensured the selections were done fairly, provided management support, and defended the recommendations of the committees in the Board of Trustees. The Board of Trustees reviewed the recommendations endorsed by the larger body. It was understood that the Trustees could only turn down recommendations if they substantively find them wanting. The Board then informed the Emperor of the selected recipients. During my service in the Trust, the period my treatment of the Trust in this book covers, there were a few instances where the Emperor had reservations about the recommendations. He expressed them openly but, after explanations of the procedures and of the care taken in the selection by the committees, he accepted all the recommendations.

In our first year, one award was the source of contention during the course of my tenure. In this instance, the committees recommended that two individuals jointly receive an award because their contributions were more or less comparable. The Emperor felt that one of them should be recognized first for he considered him to be more deserving. Before he even expressed reservations about the selection to the Trustees, he summoned me to his office and challenged the recommendation that the two be awarded simultaneously.

The question he fired as soon as I entered his office took me completely by surprise.

"Isn't Kegnazmatch Dehne your father?" the Emperor asked rhetorically.

"He is my grandfather, Your Majesty," I replied. My grandfather was alive at the time and was known to him.

"Are you aware it was Kegnazmatch who chaired the committee that did the major work that the Trust wants to attribute to one of the persons you are recommending?" he challenged.

"The selection committee has checked into the work done by the committee Your Majesty is referring to and we understood that it was established to gather information and write about palace and court procedures. Yes, we learnt that Kegnazmatch Dehne was indeed the chairman of the committee. When the committee started work, it was informed that the candidate we have recommended had already done the work. The committee saw a copy of the unpublished work and decided to disband recommending that the individual be given help to defray the cost of publication. Our selection committee was satisfied that the author did do all the work on his own and before the committee was established, I explained, confident in the careful and objective selection the respective sub-committee has made.

The Emperor did not pursue the matter further with me, nor did I convince him that both the selected candidates be recognized together as recommended. I left with the distinct impression that he favored one of them, though he was not against awarding the second in another year. He talked to the chairman of the Board of Trustees who convened a meeting of the Trustees. The Board on its own had initially held the same view as the Emperor, but had reluctantly agreed to recognize the two nominees together. The Emperor's reservations made it easy for them to revert to their own initial preference and decided that only one of the two be awarded in the first year.

The selection committees also revisited the case and went along with the recognition of one nominee on condition that the second nominee was awarded the next year. The Emperor gave the award the next year to the second nominee. Had the Trust insisted on the initial proposal, I believe the Emperor would have accepted, despite his misgivings, the joint awarding of the individuals. I used this particular case on a later occasion to explain the very basic principle that the Trust must adhere to be accepted as a credible institution.

"There may be instances when Your Majesty may not like or agree to the Trust's selections. In such cases, Your Majesty may wish to declare your disagreement with the selections but still give the awards to the recommended candidates. The Trust is, as provided in its Charter, a fully independent organization. It needs to act and be seen as one. Your Majesty established it to function independently like the Nobel Foundation and other organizations set up with the same purposes," I elaborated. I threw in the example of the Nobel Foundation to add weight to my argument. The Prize Trust had selected the Nobel Foundation for the special award named after the late Empress Menen among the first group of recipients. This prestigious foundation obviously deserved the award and its acceptance of the prize from the Trust was recognition of the Trust's raison d'être and acceptance as a credible foundation. He made no comment but he listened attentively. The Chairman of the Board of Trustees who was there on other business stressed that the various committees can be relied upon fully since they do careful and fair screening.

I left the Emperor's office at the same time as the Chairman did. In the adjoining hall, he stopped another senior trustee who was about go in to see the Emperor and told him something that greatly surprised me.

"Do you know what this young man said to His Majesty? He told His Majesty not to interfere in the work of the Prize Trust!" the Chairman said to him, pointing at me. The trustee commented that I was right because the Prize Trust has a charter and established procedures that provide for full independence. He emphasized that this was in the long-term interest of the organization.

What amazed me was the significant interpretation given to a simple explanation of the established procedures we followed to ensure fairness, confidence, and credibility in the work of the Prize Trust. If the Emperor understood what I said in that manner, neither did he say so nor show it. I believe that he saw merit in the explanations given.

No Award by Petition

In a second case, the Emperor raised the complaints of a well-known farmer and businessman. The individual complained to the Emperor that his enterprise was unfairly denied an award. The concerned individual did not get in contact with the Trustees or the Secretariat. Even if he did, we would not have discussed or explained the decision to him. The Emperor called a meeting with the Board of Trustees and began the meeting by addressing me directly, saying, and "We have received a complaint about you. The individual who is complaining claims that you prevented his getting the award in agriculture. He believes that he is deserving, but he was not selected because you opposed his candidacy." He then picked the letter of complaint and extended his hand to give it to me. But the Chairman who was closest to him took the letter and read it and passed it on to the next Trustee.

The letter was still being passed from one to the next when the Chairman started explaining that the selection was done by the committees and it was not the Director or the Trustees who made the selections. The other members also elaborated focusing on the process. I explained that the sub-committee concerned had thoroughly reviewed all the potential candidates. I pointed out that the members of the relevant selection committee had even anonymously visited the petitioner's enterprise.

Award Winners 1965:
Left to right: Ato Gebre Kirstos Desta (Fine Arts), Dedjazmach Giliagaber on behalf of the Eritrean
Children Education Association (Humanitarian), Balambaras Maheteme Selassie Wolde Maskal (Amharic
Literature), Mr. T. Camerino on behalf Manufatura Sacchi (Industry), and Professor Wolf Leslau
(Ethiopian Studies).

The second most senior Trustee, Ato Yilma Deressa, surprisingly said nothing until the very end. In a very measured tone, he posed a rhetorical question to the Emperor, 'Your Majesty, is an award given because one petitions?"
The remark had the intended impact; the petition was inappropriate. We could hear our own breathing, for there was such a total silence after his remark. The Emperor simply said that he wanted us to know of the complaint and broke up the meeting. Although he expressed his doubts in some other cases, he did not, while I was director, force the Trust to shelve duly processed recommendations.

The Nobel Prospect

In 1967, in response to an invitation by the Nobel Foundation, I was designated to go as the Director of the Prize Trust to attend the Nobel Award Ceremonies . After my visit to the Nobel Foundation and attendance at the impressive occasion, I went to report to the Emperor, because my report was expected, but also because the Emperor has shown keen interest. My request for an audience was quickly received. When I entered the Emperor's office, I noticed there were several officials in the room. Assuming they were on business unrelated to mine, I reported briefly on the event and my informative visit to the Foundation. I also reported that King Gustav had asked about the Emperor's well being and made it a special point to extend his very best wishes. Although there were a few questions by the individuals present about the ceremony and the winners, the main question centered on a rumor that some personalities in Europe had suggested the Emperor as candidate for the Nobel Peace Prize. One official who should have known that candidatures for the Nobel Prizes were confidential pointedly asked me what I have heard about the Emperor's candidature, adding that there was mention about this possibility in some papers.

"Yes, I have heard about some mention of this story. But I heard nothing in Stockholm. I could not raise it either because it would not have been appropriate for two reasons. One was that all the work on nominations and selections for awards is very confidential and was not discussed outside the selecting body. Secondly, the selection for the Peace prize is not done by the Foundation or in Sweden. The Norwegian Nobel Committee whose members are appointed by the Norwegian Parliament carries out this task," I explained.

The official who posed the question was not very happy with my reply. He must have expected me to do some lobbying or come back with some hopeful news. The official continued stressing that it will be advisable to keep close watch on the question. The Emperor was attentively listening to our exchanges and finally remarked that the Nobel Peace Prize was given only to one black man. I pointed out that the Peace Prize was given to two black men, Reverend Martin Luther King and the South African Chief Albert Luthuli, and stressed again the confidential nature of the selection process, underscoring that we in the Prize Trust were also trying to emulate the practices of the Nobel Foundation.

There were people in and outside the country that did believe the Emperor deserved consideration for the Peace Award. They cited as reasons his role in mediating the internal conflicts in the Sudan, Nigeria and North Africa, his track record since the League of Nations, his support to the United Nations, and his constructive role in African regional issues and politics.

I left the meeting convinced that the Emperor appreciated the need for confidentiality and respect for the Nobel procedures and that he would be pleased if this respected institution recognized him for his lifetime efforts. Who would not be pleased?

5

The Headaches of Land Disputes

The Prize Trust started in a temporary office in the then Haile Selassie I University in 1962, though gazetted later, to encourage excellence and to recognize outstanding achievements in selected areas. Aside from what one would consider birth pangs of an inchoate organization, the Trust faced many disputes related to the land properties it was given as sources of income.

The disputes arose from actions taken before the Emperor gave three estates to the Prize Trust. Like the Trust, some influential individuals were also given land from the Emperor's estates. Unfortunately, the transfers to these individuals were not finalized when the Trust took over its share. These individuals tried to get more or better land adjoining their holdings. They were convinced that the Trust, as a new organization, could be bulldozed into meeting their demands. The claimants focused on the importance of holding the properties because they viewed them as personal gifts from the Emperor. The cases cited illustrate the manner in which the Emperor resolved the delicate conflict between his foundation and the claims of individuals very close to him.

The Prize Trust management could not comply with the numerous claims and give away chunks of land from properties that were properly transferred to the Trust. So, anticipating such claims, we had retained a British consultant at the time of the transfer to do a survey and demarcate the boundaries of the Trust's ownership. The resultant document, which clearly indicated boundaries between the Trust properties and those given to individual owners, was accepted by the Trust and the transferring authority, namely the Emperor's estate administration. Still, ignoring the clear demarcations established and because of their access to the Emperor, claimants took their untenable contentions to the Emperor, rather than to the Board of Trustees. The Emperor had to rule on the disputes. I was frequently called to his office to answer queries and defend the interests of the Trust. The following examples cited below give an idea of how the Emperor handled such situations and the specific disputes. The disputes also showed in a concrete way the degree of obsession with land ownership.

A particularly unpleasant dispute involved a very important personality who was given about 160 hectares of land from the Tibila estate before the transfer. The Trust was informed during the handover where these hectares were located. They were not included in the properties we have taken over. Wrongly assuming that the Trust would not challenge their claims, the family tried to take different adjoining Trust land considered important for the development of the Trust's farm as a whole. The land in question bordered the Awash River.

The claimant's representative ordered workers to move in and start clearing the disputed area, thereby precipitating a confrontation. When the farm management of the Trust would not allow such an action, the claimant brought the dispute to the attention of the Emperor. As usual in such cases, I was called to the Palace without a clear sense of the reason, though I suspected that it had to do with this particular dispute. The claimant's attorney had come to see me a few days before and inquired if I had authorized the farm staff to chase out their workers. When I told the attorney I had authorized the staff, he threateningly asked me if I knew "whom I was dealing with and whether I knew of the consequences." I assured him that I gave the instructions and I did not care for the standing of his employer. He stomped out of the office, threatening quick action.

Indeed, there stood the distinguished claimant standing a few feet from the Emperor, as I was ushered into the Emperor's office. The Emperor was seated at his desk on both sides of which stood four other senior people.

As I expected, the Emperor asked, "Why did you refuse to hand over the land we gave to ...?," he asked in a firm but calm voice.

"Your Majesty," I replied, "the Trust did not refuse to hand over the property given. Our disagreement with the honorable claimant is on what land he wants to take. The claimant wants to take prime land adjoining an important water source and given to the Trust. We cannot give any land that is bordering a water source. If we do, we will be at the mercy of the claimant when we want to utilize the water from the river. We will not be able to develop the large property Your Majesty gave for the benefit of the public. Your Majesty, it is basically a question of which comes first: the interest of the public or that of an individual?"

"Are we to be insulted by him? Does it mean that we do not care about the interest of the public because we claim what is given to us by Your Majesty? How can he say that?" he asked fuming and glaring at me.

The Emperor shot back, "You must realize that he is here as the person responsible for the Prize Trust and to defend its interests. He is not benefiting personally. He is not getting an inch of land for himself. He is also right in saying that We gave the property to the Prize Trust for the benefit of the people and the public. The development of the properties for this purpose comes first."

Silence hung in the air. Like the other people present, I was surprised by the Emperor's rebuke, though I was pleasantly surprised. After a slight pause, the Emperor turned to me and asked, "What can be done? We have given a gift. We can not go back on Our word."

He understandably wanted to keep his promise to give the 160 hectares without damaging the long-term development of the Trust properties.

Hoping that the Emperor would find in my suggestion as a way out, I replied, "The Trust had not, nor does it have any problem now, with handing over 160 hectares, including eighty hectares that the honorable claimant is already cultivating. We can give the balance of eighty hectares but not land adjoining the river, for the reasons I gave earlier."

"Do that then. You hand over 160 hectares in total. Eighty will be those they are currently cultivating. You will decide which additional eighty they will have. We want this decision implemented speedily," the Emperor instructed with finality, maintaining his full support of the Trust.

The Compromise that Never Was

Another official was given eighty hectares again before the Trust came into existence. A small canal divided the Trust, and the land given to the individual. The dispute with him once again involved access to water. The claimant wanted to have land on both sides of the irrigation canal that determined the boundaries between his land and the Trust properties. He capitalized on his direct access and took the issue to the attention of the Emperor. The canal was built, utilized, and maintained by the Emperor's Estate Office and, since transfer, by the Trust.

I was summoned to see the Emperor, who was visibly upset when I entered his office. He told me of the individual's complaint and curtly asked me to explain. I used the map drawn during the initial transfer of properties to the Trust and showed him the agreed boundaries and the location of the eighty hectares of the individual. Despite the map and my extensive explanation, the Emperor remained unconvinced.

Ato Yilma Deressa, a Trustee, happened to be present. He had a special and effective approach to put his point across to the Emperor. "Your Majesty, I have a compromise solution. There is a natural boundary that should be followed. This small canal that the Trust owns should divide the properties. If this is done, there will be no more disputes," he suggested.

He traced the boundary by starting from the opposite end from where I had started; otherwise, his proposal was the same as I explained.

He spoke as if he were an objective and neutral arbiter rather than a Trustee. To my surprise, the Emperor, who was reluctant to rule against the Trust but at the same time did not want to let down the claimant, saw the compromise was a way out. He accepted the proposal, though I could not tell if he agreed because he did not realize that the supposed compromise was really no compromise or because he simply wanted the dispute to go away.

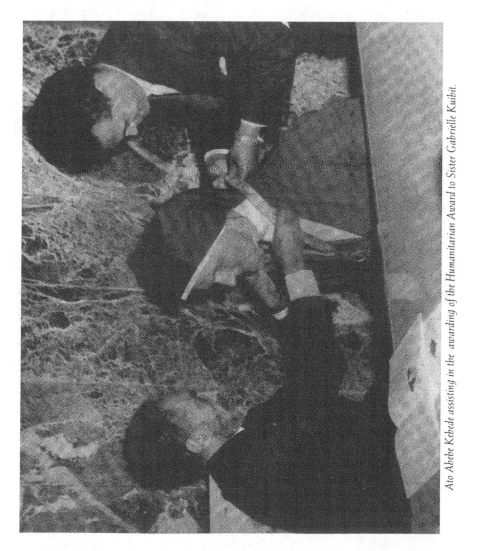

Ato Abebe Kebede assisting in the awarding of the Humanitarian Award to Sister Gabrielle Kuibit.

As the Trustee and I left the Emperor's office, he turned to me with a good-natured smile and said, "How did you like my new proposal?"

"I am surprised. It was the same thing that I was saying," I said.

"Yes, it was. But mine was *called a compromise!*" he laughed.

"Thank you very much. I hope Your Excellency will be present to offer other compromises when similar disputes arise in the future," I said appreciating the help that he gave me in a dispute that the Trust would have probably lost. Incidentally, he in several meetings I attended made very brief but cutting interventions that helped end protracted debates or explanations. He would keep unusually quiet during a discussion and at the very end make a brief suggestion or comment that the Emperor often accepted. He did the same in this case. He was reputed to be adept in this skill that he has often deployed to make effective interventions.

Soon after the settlement of the above dispute another one followed. A retired official, well known to the Emperor, had leased 80 hectares from the Estate Administration before the transfer of the Tibila properties. The Trust recognized the status of the lease, which was still in force when it took over the property. The lessee surprised us when he asked the Emperor to give him the property, claiming the land was not given to the Trust and that it was still in the custody of the Estate Administration.

When I was told to come to the Emperor's Office, I was not told why, thus unable to take any relevant documentation. I knew why when I saw a representative of the Estate Administration and the petitioner already there. The Emperor did not relish yet another land dispute. I sensed that this was going to be rough going.

"We have received a petition from ...requesting us to give him the eighty hectares he is now farming and, we are told, it is still Our property. Is there a problem?" he asked me anticipating an objection.

"Your Majesty, the property belongs to the Prize Trust and the official has only a lease for a few years. The property involved was transferred together with the lease to the Trust when we took over. We respect the current lease and, when it expires, we will decide on what is to be done," I answered.

"This is not correct. Our Administration has never transferred the leased property and it is still Your Majesty's property," the representative emphatically replied.

"We have a document signed by both the Trust and Estate Administration clearly indicating that the property was transferred to the Trust. I did not bring the document because I did not know I was called regarding this subject," I said.

"There is no such document. I never signed such a document and he cannot produce it," the representative countered with visible irritation.

"I did not say that you signed the document. Another authorized representative signed all transfer documents. Your Majesty, may I be permitted to get the document from my office?" I responded.

"Are you certain you can produce such a signed document?" the Emperor asked.

"Yes, Your Majesty. I have the document in my office."

"Bring the document later and show it to ... " He referred to the Head of his Secretariat. He had concluded that I would not say I have a document that I cannot produce. He then turned to the representative with anger and the harshest words I heard from him.

I later handed a copy of the signed agreement to the Head of the Emperor's Secretariat

Foreigners also used backdoor channels to influence the Emperor to intervene on their behalf. One blatant example involved two investors who wanted to lease the Tibila farm offering a substantial annual fee. A look into their worth by the National Bank revealed that they had hardly any capital. This fact not withstanding, the individuals managed to use an official to inform the Emperor that the Prize Trust management was, despite a good offer on their part, unwilling to give them the lease depriving the Trust of significant potential income. The official approached the Emperor while he was on a visit in Asmara.

On the same day after the Emperor returned to the capital, I was called to come to the Jubilee Palace and the Emperor asked me why we were rejecting a lease proposal for the Tibila farm by potential good investors. I explained that leasing the farm was what the Trust wanted, but the individuals who have approached us had neither capital nor past experience and involvement in agriculture. The National Bank had checked their worth and they had only about $20000 between them. They did not qualify in all respects. The Emperor accepted the explanations.

Within minutes after I returned to my office one of the potential investors phoned me:

"Good afternoon. I understand you saw His Majesty," he rhetorically asked.

"I did," I confirmed.

"We can now go ahead and agree with a lease and our offer," he confidently continued.

"No. We cannot. I informed His Majesty that we have checked into your background and worth. We have found that you do not have the capital or experience. His majesty accepted our explanation and decision," I informed him. He stayed on the line for a while and then hung up. The individual even knew the precise time when the Emperor took up the issue with me.

Tadesse's Abet! Abet!

Traditionally, citizens present to the Emperor their grievances by handing petitions whenever they could get his attention. Citizens forced the Emperor's car to stop by prostrating themselves or running to his car with petitions, shouting "Abet! Abet! Janhoy!" meaning "Hear me! Hear me, Your Majesty." Although the security guards prevented many from coming close to him, many petitioners caught the eye of the Emperor, who often instructed his aides to receive the petitions. Sometimes, the Emperor spoke to the individuals on the spot and gave follow-up instructions. Because of increased reliance on the court system and because of security concerns, such traditional open access to air grievances was largely discontinued.

We resorted to this traditional practice to bring the complaint of Tadesse, a Trust employee, to the attention of the Emperor. Tadesse had served long at the Tibila farm; he was responsible for security and prevention of encroachments on the large properties of the Trust. His was a sensitive assignment because it pitted him against the staff of senior officials who were determined to take more land and choice land. Tadesse dutifully defended the Trust's interests.

Some of those who had claims against the Trust at the Tibila farm designed a mischievous scheme by which they told the local police that Tadesse was responsible for a small landowner's death. They reported to the police that he had forced the farmer to sign over his land and then killed him. The police were trying to arrest him on this allegation but he managed to elude them and came to Addis Ababa. When we knew of the Emperor's planned visit to the Tibila farm, we agreed that he present his case by shouting the traditional "Abet! Abet!" and I would ask the Emperor to hear his complaint. We also agreed that he stay close to me and be visible so that the police do not quietly arrest him. We took him back to the farm from the capital on the day of the Emperor's visit.

When the visit was over and the Emperor was getting in his car to leave, Tadesse shouted loudly "Abet! Abet!"

The Emperor asked me what his complaint was about. Conveying to the Emperor the gist of the situation, I recommended that the staff member himself present his case. The Emperor signaled the employee to do so. As soon as Tadesse started, a very senior aide to the Emperor came forward and earnestly argued, "Your Majesty, this is police matter and under investigation. Your Majesty should not be bothered with this."

The Emperor stared at him angrily and said, "Who gave the police the authority to arrest people without sufficient proof and court order? You go ahead and present your case," he told the beaming staff member.

Tadesse explained that he had cared for an old farmer who had tuberculosis until the latter's death. The farmer had given him a plot of land in appreciation. There was also a doctor's certificate establishing tuberculosis as the cause of death. But the police, believing the allegation that he has murdered the farmer, were trying to arrest him.

The Emperor asked if I had seen the death certificate. I confirmed and took the certificate from my colleague, and showed it to the Emperor, adding that our employee was being persecuted because he was defending the interests of the organization.

"As long as you are convinced of his honesty and can vouch for him, he will be protected. Nobody should harass him and you report to Us if anybody gives him any trouble," the Emperor instructed me.

The matter ended there and the jubilant Tadesse shouted," Long live Janhoy! Long Live Your Majesty!" He turned to the entourage, directing his remark at the accusers and the police, rubbing his triumph in by shouting, "Nobody will unjustly prosecute me now! No body!"

We did not endear ourselves to the officials involved, and they left without thanking us for our hospitality, which included a rather sumptuous lunch at the farm.

A Day at Erer Gotta Citrus Farm

The Emperor's visits to the Trust farms also resulted in interesting incidents, including small demonstrations by petitioners and spontaneously organized traditional ethnic dances. For the Trust, his visits had their touchy and sensitive moments, due to the never-ending claims to get land from the organization's holdings. Claimants ensured that the Emperor was briefed on their claims, so he sometimes arrived at the farms negatively disposed.

The Emperor harbored a sentimental attachment to the Erer Gotta fruit farm in Harargue and showed continued interest in it, even after he donated it to the Prize Trust. The farm and a small livestock herd were all given to the Trust on its establishment. He visited the farm whenever he came to the nearby city, Harer, for his annual retreat. This property that was passed on to him from his father had a small villa that he used for rest during his visits. As soon as the Trust took over, the villa was converted to a small hotel for overnight customers with food provided at a small restaurant run by the farm. His bedroom was however left for his use only, despite the temptation to capitalize on the name by renting it out.

We welcomed the Emperor's continued interest and his visits, but, at times, his keen interest led him to become overly concerned and to listen to misinformation. On one occasion, the Emperor paid a surprise visit to the farm at the suggestion of a junior provincial official who had a land dispute with the Trust. The official claimed land that our farm manager and staff rightly argued was part of the property given to the Prize Trust. To win his claim, he concocted a clever scheme, using his connections to inform the Emperor that the fruit farm was in a shambles and that he should pay an unannounced visit. In the meantime, the gentleman planned to use the visit to submit a petition, requesting that the land in dispute be given to him. We learned of the Emperor's planned visit through the goodwill of the telephone exchange operator of the town where the farm was located.

The operator had heard not only of the Emperor's visit but also of the planned petition. He was thoughtful and concerned enough to alert us.

I took the train in the evening and arrived at Erer very early in the morning. We drove a few kilometers to the outskirts of the farm and waited for the Emperor's arrival. The imperial motorcade stopped when the Emperor saw us waiting on the side of the road and he addressed me.

"Where did you come from? How come you are here?" he asked with surprise and a knowing smile. He was informed his visit was going to be unannounced.

"How can I not be here when Your Majesty is honoring us with a visit?" I replied respectfully and with an equally meaningful smile.

"We are here to visit the farm," he commented. I assured him that we were ready for the visit. He proceeded to his former villa, rested for a while, and we took him on a tour of the various sections of the farm.

At the first stop, the Israeli employee in charge of livestock at the farm started to explain some of the work he and colleagues have done. He explained that he had just completed the construction of a barn and has been busy with the cultivation of cattle feed during the preceding six months. He continued, explaining that the barn and the plots of feed the Emperor was seeing were new and that they would give a good yield when the Emperor interrupted,"What do you mean new? These plots were here last year!"

Somewhat startled by the remark and the tone, the expert elaborated, "They are new and the area was cleared and seeds planted during the last few months."

"There is nothing new here. Everything was here last year," the Emperor insisted. I was doing the interpreting into Amharic, and, before I told my colleague about the last remark, I confirmed that the plots were indeed new and the expert and the colleagues with him prepared the plots and grew the feed.

My Israeli colleague could tell that I was unsuccessfully trying to convince the Emperor that the work done was new. He moved closer to the Emperor, opened his hands covered with bruises and scars, and exploded:

"How can His Majesty say the work we did in the last seven months is not new? Please tell His Majesty to look at my hands and that of my co-workers. How could he have seen something which did not exist?"

"What is he saying?" the Emperor asked, rather surprised by our colleague's visibly unsettled reaction.

As tactfully as I could and concerned that the expert's excited reaction may anger the Emperor, I explained that he showed his hands to Your Majesty to prove that he did the work himself with the laborers. I added that he was unhappy because Your Majesty was not convinced that he and his colleagues did the work.

"Let us proceed," the Emperor said rather coolly. We walked to a new barn, which the same gentleman has built during the year.

When we got to the barn, the expert explained politely:

"This is a new barn and I hope His Majesty will agree that it was not here last year! I think this could serve as a model. The feed is stored up close to the ceiling and it can be lowered whenever needed. The feed will be kept clean there, and there will be little waste," he explained.

"Yes, this is a new barn, and it is well-designed," the Emperor confirmed after he listened carefully to my verbatim interpretation. He took time to look around and listen to the presentation. When we finished, he asked me to tell the expert that "the work he has done is very good and he should continue to do so." It was obvious that the Emperor had realized that he had been given misinformation about the state of the farm. His positive remarks revealed this recognition.

We then took him to a new project site, which was becoming the pride of the farm management. On flat land with some shrubbery, the site gave one the feeling of infinity, for the plain seemed endless. The site was virgin land, mainly inhabited by wild pigs and bordered on one side by the small Erer River. A pilot activity, using some of the river's water for irrigation, had begun, and two senior college engineering students did a good job building a small canal to draw water. As a result, we had in a short time a new large area with maize and sorghum in less than a year.

The farm manager briefed the Emperor on the plan to eventually develop it into a new citrus farm. I added that university students had been employed during their long summer vacation to help us. He showed great interest in this fact and urged us to recruit more students for different activities.

The Emperor's negative tone at the start of the visit had turned complimentary. Before he left, he told our farm management people – three Israelis, one Alemaya Agricultural College graduate and administrative officers – that he was pleased with the work being done and looked forward to see even better results on his next visit. When the mischievous claimant submitted his petition during the visit, the Emperor rightly directed the petition to the Governor of the province and the courts for resolution.

During the same visit, we solved a problem that had been a headache for the farm. A magnificent bull, given to the Emperor by his son-in-law, remained on the farm after the Trust took over the property. The Trust continued to care for it until, it was hoped, the Ministry of the Palace took custody. The bull's maintenance proved costly and we asked the Ministry, again and again, to take it or pay for its upkeep. The officials made light of our pleas and argued that the Trust was being fussy and ungrateful in complaining about such a small cost when the Emperor had given his whole estate. Our argument that the Ministry had a budget and for such things and it should defray our cost fell on deaf ears.

In the end, we decided to slaughter the bull on the occasion of the Emperor's visit, thereby accomplishing two tasks: dispose of the costly bull and provide a luncheon for the imperial entourage and guests. This was a touchy option, because the bull was a special gift to the Emperor, and we did not ask for permission. After the lunch, the members of the entourage complimented us for the excellent meat served and we quietly enjoyed the compliments, without letting them know that we had served them our big headache.

A few months letter, I got a call from the Ministry of the Palace requesting we hand over the celebrated bull. When I told the official that the bull had been put to good and honorable use, he could not believe that we had taken such action without authorization and stressing that the bull was a gift to the Emperor by a family member. Reminding him of our efforts to hand over the bull and explaining we did not have any other fitting means of honoring the visit, I assured him of our good intentions and, if necessary, I would explain our action to the Emperor. He realized the Ministry's failure to act earlier would put his Ministry on the defensive. Our conversation ended politely but abruptly. Neither the Ministry of the Palace nor did the spirit of the celebrated animal ever came back to haunt the farm.

A few months later, another case of misinformation about Erer farm led to urgent summons to the Palace. I was told that I had to see the Emperor right away. I was rushed into his office, and when I arrived, a member of the Executive Committee of the Trust was present. I noticed a look of concern on the latter's face.

"Good morning," began the Emperor. "We were informed by a senior official, who was at the Erer Gota farm last week that the fruit crop was not being harvested on time and consequently fruit was rotting on the ground. We are told that one sees fallen oranges all over the farm. What seems the problem?" the Emperor asked, in a measured tone, making it clear he trusted his informant.

"If the visit to the farm took place last week, what the official told Your Majesty is impossible," I replied coolly despite my anger at the individual who had told such nonsense.

"What do you mean by impossible? Explain."

"It is not possible because there are no fruits to pick at this time of the year! Harvest time is a couple of months away. Only two weeks ago, the Palace wanted to buy fruits from the farm to send to the President of Turkey. Our staff had great difficulty to fill a couple of baskets to accommodate the request."

Surprised by the gross misinformation he had received, he kept quiet for a while. As if he were talking to himself, he asked, "What do they get out of misleading Us?"

We found out from the farm management who visited the farm during the days in question. When I told the gentleman that it would have been easier and helpful to call the Trust and let us know of his concerns, he apologetically and frankly told me that he had reported what one gentleman had told him. He stayed at the hotel on the farm and did not visit the farm. His source of information turned out to be a local official who had a land dispute with the Trust.

Age and Sensitivity

The Emperor's visits to the farms also showed a side of the Emperor for which he was known and admired – his remarkable physical agility and strength. Any one who has seen the Emperor take one of his walks can only but admire, despite his advancing age, his remarkable endurance and the determination to show it. We were all amazed to see him walk considerable distances on the Trust estates under intense heat and against advice of his aides. The Emperor showed sensitivity to any suggestion that cast doubts on his physical capacity or any hint that age has slowed him down.

During a visit to the Tibila estate one Saturday morning the Emperor showed this sensitivity, if not resentment, to the suggestion that a taxing physical walk be avoided. The visit to the farm that was located in the Awash Valley extended to past noon when it gets searing hot and uncomfortable, even for the people who live there and are used to the heat.

We were showing him various projects, and this called for walking from section to section at different locations. Since the locations were far apart, walking on that hot day was very trying for everybody. The Emperor walked without strain, at least without showing it. The Army Chief of Staff who had accompanied the Emperor came to me and whispered in my ear, "I think you should tell His Majesty that it is better to drive to the next plot. It is too hot and far to walk." Wondering why he, a very senior official, does not make the suggestion himself, I told him that it was more fitting for him to tell the Emperor. The Chief of Staff was very quick with his "No, you should tell him. It will be more appropriate since he is your guest!"

Rather reluctantly, I said to the Emperor, "The next stop for visit is quite far. It may be better to go by car."

The Emperor glared at me, clearly surmising that I was telling him that he was not strong enough to walk long distances. His reply was quick.

"Why can We not walk there? You think We can not walk far!"

We only continued walking a short distance, however, when he changed his mind and headed towards his car, and I thought, "No wonder the Chief of Staff told me it was my duty as host to discourage such a walk!"

One other incident that took place when the construction of our offices was in progress is hard to forget. At the time, the Trust was located in temporary offices in the then Haile Selassie University, awaiting a move to our new offices. One late afternoon, we were alerted that the Emperor had just been at the University and was coming to our office.

"When are you going to have your new offices? This is not adequate," he said, as soon as he walked in and acknowledged our bows of greeting.

"We hope within one or two months. The owners of the building where our new office will be have assured us that they will give priority to the completion of the construction of our office-to-be," I explained.

"How much have they progressed? Let us go and see what is being done. What else do you need?" he asked as he started towards the exit door. I told him that I was finalizing our budget and we need to have some cash for daily operations. He turned to an aide and, with a nod, indicated that aide should take note.

We had hardly recovered fully from his unexpected appearance when we had to rush to the building where our offices would be housed, and, from a distance, I pointed out which part of the building would constitute the office. He listened attentively, and, when I finished, he walked to the temporary wooden structure the workers used to go up and down carrying construction material. The contraption had neither stairs nor railings to hold on. The ramp was narrow in width and understandably full of clutter, cement drops and paint. We all thought that he was getting close to have a better look. Instead, he proceeded to climb up the temporary structure while those around stood aghast, shocked that he would take such a risk. The chief aide-de-camp rushed to persuade him not to do so, but the Emperor gave him such a threatening look that he just stood still unsure of what to do.

A security officer and I followed. Everybody else just looked on for fear of adding too much weight. The Emperor went about seven feet and stopped apparently realizing the climb was indeed risky and messy. He looked around for a minute or so and climbed down slowly.

The Emperor visiting the Tibia Farm and enjoying a long walk despite the noon heat.

6

The Man of Faith

The Emperor benefited from the support of the influential Ethiopian Orthodox Tewahedo Church. This was true of him as it was of his predecessors. The monarchs needed the church's blessing either to ascend to or stay in power. Even governments that succeeded the Emperor, despite their avowedly non-religious orientation, indirectly ensured church support. They made certain that their own supporters, or at least individuals who would not oppose them, headed the church and filled important positions in the administration of the church. Mengistu's regime executed Patriarch Teoflos and later had benign, if not submissive, heads appointed. The Ethiopian Peoples Revolutionary Democratic Front has a strong supporter in the current Patriarch of the Ethiopian Orthodox Tewahedo Church.

Living His Faith

The Emperor, by all accounts, set an example by living his faith, respecting the practices and the institution of his church, and making generous donations. Religion was at the core of his being. His speeches and private conversations frequently mentioned God and divine guidance or protection and his "faith in divine providence is a built-in factor in his personal armory."[28] His attendance of church and participation in religious ceremonies were frequent and publicized. Both his religious convictions and the demands of the teachings of his religion markedly influenced his daily life and actions. He showed his strong religious bent in very special and ordinary ways. At church, he had no inhibitions to prostrate himself in front of the altar with humility and offer his prayers. There were times, according to members of the clergy in the churches he frequented, when they saw tears roll down his face as he prayed.

The Emperor turned to prayers in times of sadness and loss. After the defeat of the Ethiopian army at Maychew, during the retreat, the Emperor went to Lalibela Medhane Alem Church and prayed for Ethiopia's deliverance; he took a vow that he would govern Ethiopia justly. He reportedly took the defeat as a sign that God was displeased with him and the country. He attributed his return to his throne and Ethiopia's liberation as God's will and His forgiveness. A comprehensive coverage of the Emperor's contributions and his religious devotion has been presented in a church publication, Emperor Haile Selassie and the Ethiopian Church, October 2000. The publication came out on the occasion of the internment of the Emperor's remains.

Ato Kebriye Dejene, told me of an incident, which is telling of how meticulous the Emperor could be in his observance of religious practices. The Ethiopian Orthodox Tewahedo Church faithful avoid using items made, or work done on things, on identified religious days. A devoutly religious person should not consume even cereals ground on such days. The Emperor observed Saint Mary's Day. He once gave his watch to Kebriye to have it repaired, and St Mary's Day was being observed during the same week. The Emperor called Kebriye a few days later at his home and told him not to allow the repair done on Saint Mary's Day. Fortunately, the repair was already complete. When he was

---

28 Imperial Ethiopian Ministry of Information. Selected Speeches 1918-1937, Introduction,
    Minassie Haile, Artistic Printing Press, Addis Ababa, 1967.

informed of this, the Emperor remarked with apparent relief, "Good.
Had the watch been repaired on Saint Mary's Day, We would not have
worn it any more." Kebriye and others also believed that the Emperor
slept on the floor and not on his bed during the long fasting periods of
Lent and *"filsetta,"* or the 16-day period of fasting that precedes the Feast
of the Assumption of Saint Mary.

The Emperor expected others to live by the tenets of their religion
as well. He expressed so to me on the occasion of my marriage. Rahel
and I got married while I was still in the Prize Trust. I did not think it
necessary to let the Emperor know of the planned event, though I was
told that it was appropriate, if not expected, because of my association
with the Trust. I felt our wedding was not important enough to engage
his attention. Some of the Board members of the Trust we invited to
the wedding even prodded me to inform him; Abebe Kebede especially
advised that it should be mentioned to the Emperor. I later learnt Abebe
had eventually gone ahead and mentioned it to him. A few days before
my wedding, I was called to the Palace where the Emperor in a fatherly
way scolded me and gave me a wedding gift. The audience went thus:

"Good morning. When is your wedding?" he asked in a pleasant tone.

"Next Sunday, Your Majesty," I replied, surprised that I had been
called in this connection.

"Are you getting married in church?"

"Yes, at Estifanos church."

"Very good. Are you taking the Holy Communion?"

"No, Your Majesty," I replied. I felt uncomfortable anticipating a
follow-up question that will no doubt ask why not.

"If you are getting married in church, why are you not taking the
Holy Communion?" I had to think fast and give a palatable reason that
will get me off the hook.

"My fiancée will not agree to do so," I responded taking advantage
of her absence. He did not believe me.

"Why is it you young people don't take religious matters seriously?
It is surprising. Marriage is such a holy undertaking that one should

sanctify by taking communion," he commented rather disappointed. Fortunately, he did not pursue the matter further.

"We wish you a happy marriage. A small gift will be sent to you," he said ending the audience. The gift was one thousand birr.

The Emperor's religious values were tested daily in many ways; one of which was in approving death sentences. Those who advised him on cases attest that he "agonized" in deciding on death sentences because the teaching of his faith for mercy weighed heavily on him. As Head of State, he was duty-bound to sign off on death sentences after they have been processed through the judicial process. He often and repeatedly asked involved officials to assure him that the trial was fair and thoroughly conducted to justify so final an action. He struggled between his duty to sanction such recommendations and his own concern about reaching just decisions.

The hostile military regime and the Emperor's opponents hurled accusations even claiming that he had opponents murdered. The Mengistu regime took special pleasure in demonizing the Emperor yet did not provide convincing evidence that the Emperor was involved in such crimes. Had Mengistu and his cohorts any evidence to implicate him in murders, they would have had no compunction to use it to speedily try him or dispose of him. What could have been a better reason than a murder charge to use against the person they feared most? A regime that had so remorselessly killed young, old, clerics, and even its own dissenting supporters for real or concocted offenses would have jumped at the slightest evidence. With no palatable evidence, the regime instead resorted to slander, accusations of financial corruption, and vicious personal attacks. Why would the Emperor who was strong enough to deal with his opponents in other ways resort to drastic and politically harmful measures? Ato Tekle Tsadik Mekuria, Ketema Yifru and others remained convinced that such allegations were not in character with such a devoutly religious person.

The EPRDF regime has shown some restraint in publicly denigrating the Emperor. It has, however, continued to undermine his legacy through subtle means such as editing or deleting media material. It has continued to slander him and accuse him of financial corruption, and it did so a few days before the formal burial of the Emperor's remains in November 2000, no doubt to undermine the planned ceremony and discourage massive public participation.

The Emperor's preferred forms of punishment were imprisonment, more often house arrest, or distancing the person; furthermore, he has been criticized for bringing back to his fold individuals who have openly deserted or opposed him. Apart form those who died in the armed engagements, Haile Selassie's severe punitive actions against, for instance, participants of the 1960 coup were limited to a relatively few who were considered leaders. Several of the top leaders died fighting or committed suicide. Others were sentenced to prison and the once trusted top general involved was tried and hanged, in part because of pressure from the relatives of senior officials killed by the coup participants.

Ethiopia did not in her recent history experience the scale and type of brutality of the type Mengistu Haile Mariam unleashed. The Emperor would not have even contemplated, let alone resorted to, Dergue actions such as mass killings in the streets, in prison yards, and the execution of children in front of their parents, and receive payment from relatives to get the bodies of their daughters and sons.

Despite his commitment to his own religion, the Emperor respected and even allowed the spread of other faiths such as Muslim, Protestant, Catholic religions. The same cannot be said of Arab leaders of countries, which to this day do not allow Christian churches to be built in their territories.

The Emperor did favor the Ethiopian Orthodox Tewahedo Church, the state religion so identified with Ethiopian history. He did so in the same way, but less zealously, the neighboring countries favored Islam. Along with financial support to his church, the Emperor supported the church by securing the independence of the Ethiopian

Orthodox Tewahedo Church from the Coptic Church in Alexandria, by encouraging its participation in global religious bodies such as the World Council of Churches and the Oriental Orthodox Churches Conference, and by promoting the establishment of Ethiopian Orthodox Tewahedo churches abroad. His efforts took out the church of its age-old isolation.

The Emperor is deservedly credited for significantly and gradually distancing religion from government. He reduced the church's influence in state affairs while, at the same time, giving it considerable internal autonomy. He was strong enough to take drastic measures that countered the church's traditions. Among these measures were allowing foreign missionaries to operate and run schools in the country, employing educators such as the Jesuits in government schools and colleges, and encouraging tolerance and freedom of religion. The Jesuits did not wear their religious costumes while teaching or at work to avoid touching on sensitive cords. He is remembered for taking the unequivocal stand espoused in his well-known public pronouncement that "religion is individual. The country belongs to all."

Not happy with his relatively liberal approach to church and state relations, influential members of the Ethiopian Orthodox Tewahedo faith clergy have pointed out to him that the policies he has adopted undermined the Church and its efforts. Some even warned him that his stand would bring about his downfall. The late Abune Yoseph who was apparently opposed to the separation of church and state, reportedly told the Emperor that "because Your Majesty had voluntarily and in pursuance of political benefit abandoned God's country that was preserved by our gallant forefathers and adopted the policy that religion is private while the country is for all, you and the country will be destroyed. I see you being brutally killed by your own army."[29] The Emperor's response was to walk away angrily without any comment.

The Emperor believed that the age-old closeness between the

---

29 Hawarya, Volume 1, No.18, p.8.

church and the state had to be redefined, if Ethiopia, both a Christian and Moslem nation, was to avoid religious conflicts and tensions. Teferra Haile Selassie aptly assesses the importance of the need for a realistic policy when he wrote, "The emerging reality, in post-war Ethiopia, was the secular nature of the state, where members of one denomination and/or ethnic origin were not allowed to dominate the affairs of the state."[30] The Emperor and his associates had not only recognized this reality but carefully and gradually worked to bring about the realization of the transition to a secular state.

The Ras Tafarian Phenomenon

In this context, mention of the Ras Tafarian movement is relevant. This movement named after the Emperor had engaged attention for decades, and, due to Bob Marley's involvement, had sparked even greater interest in the latter part of the last century. The Ras Tafarian phenomenon, both in its spiritual and political context, is of considerable significance in Ethiopia's relationship with people of African descent in the Caribbean and in the United States.

The movement has relevance in two respects as it relates to the Emperor and Ethiopia. One is the delicate situation the Emperor found himself because of the spiritual role the Ras Tafarians ascribed to him. This role was especially advocated in the initial period of the movement's existence. He was then called a messiah and his coming to power was seen as a realization of the prophecy in Psalm 68 that "princes will come of Egypt and Ethiopia shall stretch her hands unto God." This association with Ethiopia had existed since the late eighteen century. The founding of the Ethiopian Baptist Church founded as far back as 1784 is a case in point. This Church did not reflect the teachings of the Ethiopian Orthodox Tewahedo religion, but inspired by the prophecy, nurtured a symbolic and biblical link

---

30 Haile-Selassie, Teffera. *The Ethiopian Revolution: 1974-1991 From A Monarchichal Autocracy to A Military Oligarchy.* London and New York: Kegan Paul International, 1997 p.56.

with Ethiopia.[31]

As a devout Christian, the Emperor could not accept these messianic attributes and discouraged the claim privately and publicly in no uncertain terms. In a BBC interview in 1967, he indicated that he had told Ras Tafarians that they "should never make the mistake of assuming or pretending that a human being is emanated from a deity." He was uncomfortable that the notion was ever entertained.

On the other hand, the Emperor could not ignore people who idolized him. He brought them closer by allowing missionaries from the Caribbean to come to Ethiopia and help, especially in the promotion of health and education. Emperor Menelik had already broken the ground by employing and encouraging mainly European professionals to help him and his government. Haile Selassie's encouragement resulted in an influx that totaled 150 mostly West Indian and Afro-Americans[32] living in the country and many worked in professional areas, notably as pilots, medical staff and in business. He also gave land in southern Ethiopia for those who wanted to migrate, and Ras Tafarians are still living and farming on the land.

Secondly, and perhaps just as important, bringing the teachings of the Ethiopian Church to the western hemisphere was of a special significance. The Emperor encouraged the Ethiopian Orthodox Tewahedo Church to assign priests to serve the Caribbean. This important action responded to spiritual needs and promoted appreciation of Ethiopian culture abroad. The late Abune Yishak's long and successful service in the region exemplifies this achievement.

The Emperor exerted influence among the Rastas through his personal and diplomatic gestures. One much appreciated action by the Emperor took place during his visit to Jamaica in 1966 where he received a "tumultuous welcome." The Emperor "delayed disembarking from the aero plane for an hour until Mortimer Planner, a well-known Rasta,

---

31 Lee, Helene. *The First Rasta: Leonard Howell and the Rise of Rastafarianism.* Translated Version, Chicago University Press, 2003., pp 54-55. Originally published by Flam Marion, 1999.
32 Ibid.

personally welcomed him. From then on, the visit was a success."

Even nature, the crowds believed, cooperated on the day of his arrival in Jamaica, which was suffering from a drought. It rained at the time of the Emperor's arrival.

The Emperor is especially credited with successfully modifying the thinking of the Rastas, who advocated return to Africa, to focusing first in liberating their people at home. His counsel was heeded and it gave birth to the slogan "liberation before repatriation."[33]

As William R. Scott in his *Sons of Sheba's Races* so commendably highlights, African Americans, their churces, and the people of the Caribbean have supported and identified with Ethiopia in concrete and committed manner. They demonstrated en masse and many volunteered to fight the Italian invasion of Ethiopia. They mobilized resources, albeit from a limited resource pool, and public opinion in defense of Ethiopia. People of African descent in the Caribbean and the United States, especially at the grassroots level, rallied to Ethiopia's cause by establishing new support groups, most prominently the Provisional Committee for the Defense of Ethiopia, the Friends of Ethiopia, and later the umbrella United Aid for Ethiopia. Some fought or helped directly at the battlefront. Despite its failure to influence the United Sates government to act to prevent Italian aggression, the commendable efforts of the NAACP brought the Emperor and Ethiopia closer to their brothers and sisters.[34] The Emperor and his associates, notably Dr. Martin Workeneh, Kentiba Gebru and professor Tamrat Emanuel have capitalized on this affinity to cultivate goodwill and mutually beneficial relationship with the Caribbean people and Afro-Americans. The Ras Tafarians, despite their unorthodox views and ways, have contributed to generating and sustaining interest and support for Ethiopia and its history.

---

33 Wikipedia, The Free Encyclopedia, Rastafari Movement, *Visit of Selassie I to Jamaica.*
34 Scott, William R, *The Sons of Sheba's Races*, Indiana University Press, 1993, pp.110-135.

7

On the Lighter Side

The media image of the Emperor belabored the formal and serious characteristics of his personality. Most of us consequently knew the Emperor rather than Haile Selassie, the person. His lighter, gentler-human-side has been more talked than written about. The following few episodes reveal the gentler human Emperor,

The Case of the Walking Piano

Christine Sanford tells of a predicament she and her husband faced when the Emperor, Crown Prince and Regent at the time, asked a favor. The Regent had enjoyed piano music and dancing at a dinner given by the Sandfords, so he invited them to a dinner at his residence.

Along with the invitation, the Crown Prince requested a simple favor, simple for him. He asked the Sandfords to come to the dinner with their piano so that they could have some more of the enjoyable music they had at the their earlier get-together. The transport of the piano in the absence of an appropriate vehicle was a challenge that the guests of the Regent met head on. Sandford narrates that porters were hired "to shoulder the piano, and preceded by it, we rode out to dinner and a pleasant evening of music and dancing."[35]

---

35 Sandford, Christine. *Ethiopia Under Haile Selassie*, J.M. Dent & Sons Ltd. London 1946, p.37.

Lentils Soup and Its Use

The Emperor's frequent presence in school meets and events, before the expansion of schools made it impossible, were looked at as fatherly and encouraging. Each visit generated considerable talk and students compared notes about what "shime" (the Old Man) had said to whom. One such light moment was a memorable exchange between the Emperor and a friend during one of the Emperor's suppertime visits to the then University College of Addis Ababa. The Emperor stopped at our dinner table and started a conversation with a friend who was enjoying his bowl of lentil soup.

"What are you eating?" the Emperor asked with a faint smile

"I am having lentil soup," replied the friend nervously.

"What use do lentils have for the body?"

"They have vitamins."

"What other benefits do they have?" the Emperor went on, with a broadening smile.

"I think they have vitamins," our friend repeated with discomfort.

"Is that all?" the Emperor persisted

"They make one stronger," my friend responded visibly embarrassed. He had suddenly realized what the Emperor was after. He knew the answer, but he could not say it. All of us at the table understood the situation, and enjoyed having fun at the expense of our friend. The Emperor moved on, laughing heartily, and knowing full well that all of us knew the answer. Though our friend was too embarrassed to say it, Ethiopians believe that lentils make men very virile. As soon as he left our table, the question the Emperor asked was immediately passed on to the next table and then to the next etc. The sound of laughter rippled through the hall.

We Versus I

Many jokes, some of them not so flattering, have been told about the Emperor's use of the pronoun "We" in place of the "I." It was not unusual for heads of governments or states to use the plural pronoun when the intention is to speak collectively on behalf of the cabinet or government. But in his case, he used We instead of I in his speeches and conversations, as did his predecessors and contemporary monarchs.

One morning in his office, the Emperor gave specific instructions to a senior official of his Secretariat while a young official who had not too long ago returned from studies abroad and was assigned to assist the Emperor looked on. The senior official took the instructions and left. A few days later, the same group was present when the Emperor followed up by asking the official, "What happened to the instruction We gave you a few days ago on...?"

"I do not remember receiving the instruction on this subject, Your Majesty," the official replied rather hesitantly.

"We gave this instruction a few days ago. We are sure of it," and turning to the young returnee assistant, and asking him, "didn't we tell him what should be done? Did We not give the instructions?"

"Yes we did, Your Majesty," confirmed the young assistant, innocently assuming the Emperor was using the collective rather than the imperial We! Although the Emperor may have been amused, he did not show it, and later those present and the young aide's friends had fun teasing him about such a breach of protocol and power-sharing attempt!

The Lift is for the Aged

Another incident surrounded a Prize Trust Award ceremony. A day before the ceremony, the Emperor's secretariat informed us that the President of India, who was visiting Ethiopia, would attend the ceremony as the Emperor's guest.

The Emperor arrived first and met the President at the entrance of the Africa Hall where the ceremony was to be held. The two heads of states entered and were proceeding towards the dais when an interesting gesture on the part of the Emperor caught attention. The President of India had difficulties seeing and was helped by an aide, especially going up steps to get to the dais. When they reached the steps, the President's aide came and offered him his arm. The Emperor, instants later, did the same extending his left arm on the other side to the President to lean on. The latter, though gracious in acknowledging the gesture, stuck with the stronger and more experienced arm of his officer!

We were further amused by what the Emperor did to further drive the point that he was in a fit physical condition. The award ceremony ended, and I led the way towards the lift that the two heads of state were to take on departure. The Emperor accompanied the distinguished guest to the lift and saw him off. He then turned to me and asked," what is next in the program?"

"With Your Majesty's permission, we would like a group picture of the award winners with Your Majesty outside in front of the building."

"Fine. Which way do We go?"

"The lift that His Excellency the President took goes right to the place where the picture will be taken," I suggested. The Emperor smiled yet appeared to be scolding me for the suggestion.

"The lift is for the President of India!" he said in unmistakably loud tone.

I got his message. He was strong and healthy and did not need the lift! I could not but smile understandingly.

"The steps down are at the main entrance," I quickly said and led the way back to the entrance.

The Emperor's smile got even broader when he noted that all those who were close by had heard his pointed message. He obviously relished the fact that he has put his message across not only to me but everybody near. The Emperor and the whole entourage went the longer way down the stairs.

An Officer's Redemption

The Emperor was participating in a foundation laying ceremony at Assab Airport. As a symbolic gesture to underscore the importance of the construction work and urge all to cooperate in the effort, everyone, including the Emperor were carrying chunks of rock and depositing them at a select spot where the construction was to be. The Emperor noticed a big officer carrying a small stone, and he called out to the man teasing him for not bearing a bigger load.

The embarrassed officer did not expect to be noticed, least of all by the Emperor. He quietly and, he thought unseen, went back, chose a heavy stone, and threw it on the pile. The Emperor saw this redemptive effort. The incident did not however end there. The stone broke to pieces on impact and a piece landed on the Emperor. The officer was embarrassed and shocked by what happened. The Emperor told him to ignore the harmless accident. On his return to the capital, the officer was further surprised to learn that the Emperor had given him a plot of land and money to build a home.

How Not to Fool the Emperor

The Emperor liked to go to the Air Force base at Debre Zeyt often and walk around in the compound. He struck up conversations with the cadets and personnel during these relaxed promenades. One afternoon he came across a group of cadets who on seeing him formed a line and saluted him.

"What is your name? Whose son are you?" he asked one of the young cadets who stood at attention third in the lineup, for the cadet struck a resemblance to some one the Emperor knew.

The cadet gave his name and that of his father, who was a learned individual in religious poetry or the traditional *'qene."* The Emperor knew the father well.

"You father is well-known for his *qene*. How about you? Let us have some *qene* from you," the Emperor requested the cadet, who was known among his friends for his humor and jokes.

"Yes, I can," he said threw out a bunch of words freely lumped together. He thought that he could pull a fast one on the Emperor who, unbeknown to the young man, was very familiar with *qene*. After all, the Emperor had exposure in school and has all his life been hearing the learned extemporize erudite *qene* at special occasions.

"What! You are a scoundrel!" the Emperor scolded him and walked away without further reaction.

Alden Whitman cites a story of a gentleman who thought the Emperor would not remember him from an earlier encounter. The gentleman had received a gift from the Emperor for his service during the war against the Italians. On another occasion where the Emperor was again distributing gifts to a similar group, the man approached the Emperor and claimed that he had been overlooked. The Emperor embarrassed the individual by telling him that he lied "calling the petitioner by name and citing the exact place, day and hour at which he had been rewarded for bringing a string of mules for the army."[36]

The Emperor Needed a Lift

Ato Bekele Beshah recalled how he unexpectedly ended up giving the Emperor a lift because the Emperor's car had broken down coming back to the capital from Debre Zeyt, a small town where the Emperor often went on weekends. Ato Bekele was also coming back to Addis Ababa when he saw the Emperor sitting in the imperial car, on the roadside. His entourage was standing around apparently unable to restart the car. Bekele got out of his car, saluted the Emperor, and then resumed his journey to the capital. After he drove a short distance, he

---

36 Gelb, Arthur , A.M. Rosenthal and Whitman, Alden. Haile Selassie 1892-1975, *Great Lives of The Twentieth Century*, Times Books, 1988, p.252.

saw in his rearview mirror one of the Emperor's escort cars speeding to catch up with him, and people around were signaling him to stop. The escort car caught up with him and the officer told him to go back to the Emperor. When he arrived at the scene, still unsure of what was happening, an aide opened the rear door of his car and held it for the Emperor, who calmly left his own car and settled in the back seat of Bekele's car. Bekele was asked to drive to the capital. He suddenly realized that his car has been commandeered and he has been drafted a temporary royal driver. About half way to the capital, Bekele saw coming a flag waiving royal car rushing to the rescue in response to a phone call.

The Emperor finished his journey in the more appropriate vehicle driven by his own seasoned driver. Bekele Beshah regretted that he was not allowed to continue and take the Emperor through the streets of Addis Ababa to the Palace. He would have impressed a lot of people by the unique assignment

This Seat is Taken

Emperor Haile Slelassie's love for animals was well known and it was this love for pets that was distorted and used against him when the military regime was undermining his rule and building its case for overthrowing him.

Ethiopians are very familiar with his small pet dog that went everywhere with him, as well as his lions, cheetahs, horses, and his big dogs. The small dog was somewhat of a celebrity because of a story, and it is very likely only a joke, when an official, upon completing an audience with the Emperor, was pursued by the little dog, barking and trying to bite his legs. The official reportedly said in a reverent tone and with the pronoun used to address the elderly and respected, "why don't you (*ersewo*) leave me alone?"

I also had an awkward encounter with the little pet at the Emperor's office. He had called a meeting of the Board of the Prize Trust to discuss a proposal that the Prize Trust be a language academy. An individual close to the Emperor put this proposal forward not very long after the Trust started. The Emperor apparently wanted to give the suggestion at least pro forma consideration to appease its advocates.

At the start of the meeting, the Emperor invited the members to take seats. Anticipating that the meeting will take long, chairs had already been brought in. There was however one chair short. Since we were all standing in a row on the basis of seniority, I was the last one in the line. I remained standing.

"Take a seat," the Emperor told me not realizing that there was no chair for me. He repeated his instruction.

I decided to go further back in the room and find a chair. I saw from a quick side-glance a chair near the wall. I was about to reach for it when I noticed two things. The chair was big and bulky. More interesting, the chair was already occupied. The famous pet dog was blissfully enjoying a mid-morning siesta. I quietly returned to my standing position.

The Emperor again noticed that I was still the odd man standing. He spoke again rather loudly expressing his surprise why there were not enough chairs. The deputy aide de camp that was in the hallway must have heard him for a chair was rushed in moments later. As the discussion went on, I looked back at the chair that I had intended to use. It had a crown carved on top. It was one of the chairs used by the Emperor. I was glad that I did not give the impression, thanks to the relaxing pet, that I had any aspirations to the throne.

Two friends told me of the Emperor's reaction when they, on separate occasions, noticed that the little dog climbing all over the Emperor, covering his dark suit with hair. They both tried to use their handkerchiefs to dust off the hair from his suit. To each, the Emperor remarked, "Do not bother. This is what one with love for animals has to live with."

How to Safeguard the Emperor from a Stampede

A few days before a trip to the Nobel Prize Ceremony, I had to see the Emperor, as is customary, before my departure. I was asked to be present at the Ghion Hotel grounds. The Emperor frequently went there after five o'clock to visit his horses housed in a stable on the hotel grounds.

I saw him come from the adjoining Jubilee Palace to the hotel grounds, walking briskly and with a fairly large entourage. He was talking business with two officials and, when they finished, I was presented. He asked what the program looked like and what my expectations were. I stressed that, since the Prize Trust was a new organization with basically the same broad purpose of recognizing excellence, I should learn a lot that could be useful to our work.

As I was offering my comments, I saw an assorted pack of animals rushing straight at the Emperor. I thought they were about to run him over so I instinctively raised a file folder that I was holding, and using it as a stick, started to steer them away from him. I heard him say from behind me, amused and laughing, "It is alright! Leave them alone!"

To my surprise, the security and all the others present did not move an inch but watched my actions with amusement. They have seen this eager rush of the animals before. I moved back and watched the animals crowd the Emperor; some of them were nudging him. Palace employees came quickly with a tray of green chickpeas and other green feed, which the Emperor gave to the animals. He was happily responding to their earnestness to take the feed from his hands. He scolded the over-zealous and fairly distributed some to each.

At one point, he started looking around and asked, "Where is the donkey?" Some one pointed out that it was coming, and we all looked at the direction that he pointed. A limping donkey was approaching as fast as it could. The Emperor walked towards the donkey with the chickpeas, gently touched its head, and started feeding it.

I learned that he had bought the donkey from a farmer who had heavily loaded it with produce that he was taking to the market. The

Emperor, upon seeing the handicapped donkey struggling with the load, stopped his car, paid for the donkey and the load, and had the donkey transported to his Palace.

He then moved towards the horses' stable, where he again received a warm welcome from the horses that started neighing and making loud noises. They recognized him, as well as the special treat that they knew he brought.

After my competition from the animal kingdom was over, the rather informal audience ended, and I took my leave. My attempts to show my valor and protect the person of the Emperor from a great stampede had ended without national attention.

It is a tragic irony the love the Emperor had for animals was unfairly used in 1974 to depict him as a callous autocrat who fed his dogs good beef while his people were dying. A decade later, his accusers ended up responsible for the unimaginable death of a million people. They were celebrating with imported champagne when so many were perishing.

The Embarrassing Footage

The takeover by the military regime and the vicious propaganda against the Emperor generally created fear, and uncharacteristic behavior. A few former loyalists denounced his rule and renounced titles and recognition that were conferred upon them to avoid persecution or to ingratiate themselves with the new rulers. Other former officials, though critical of some aspects of his rule, gave him due credit and quietly nurtured admiration. To this day, many honored and savored titles conferred on them by the Emperor. Many more kept their feelings to themselves and went along with their professional work and survival under Mengistu's brutal regime.

Some innocuous and amusing situations arose due to lingering respect for the late Emperor conflicting with the adverse political climate against his rule.

A friend, who had been a former official under the Emperor,

became an ambassador at an important duty station by appointment of the military regime. He had invited several friends and me to dinner at his residence, and the party included some middle-level officials of the regime who had come from the capital for an international meeting. A few of the staff from the embassy were also present. Such a mix meant that conversations were guarded, especially where the Emperor or the Dergue and its work were concerned. There was reluctance to speak about the Emperor, unless it was to disparage him or criticize his rule.

The television was on, and a documentary on some of personalities of recent times was being shown. Rather unexpectedly, a brief footage depicting the Emperor came on the screen. The footage showed him in his tan military uniform. His familiar "enigmatic" smile, his graceful and royal wave filled the screen. The enthusiastic crowd cheering him was all there for us to relive a spectacle that we had all witnessed for years but that was no longer allowed on television in Ethiopia.

Every eye was glued to the screen. When the scene ended, an awkward silence followed. Nobody knew what to say in the midst of such a mixed group with different political outlooks.

"I think I just had a glimpse of the Emperor on the screen!" said the ambassador taking a non-committal stand. He wanted to break the silence. We all laughed heartily at this subtle and amusing effort both to remark on what happened but at the same time to remain non-committal. The laughter had hardly subsided when one of the friends present remarked in jest that he hoped there would be no press statement from the Embassy denying the footage was ever seen in the residence.

There was guarded conversation about the footage televised, essentially confined to non-committal exchanges about when and where the footage was taken. The exchanges were benign and reserved because of the presence of Dergue officials from the capital. This was a time when in Ethiopia citizens were persecuted for even possessing the Emperor's photographs.

8

Progressive or Obstructive

Testimonies of Some Associates

A progressive leader, for most of his life, a "radical" in his early years, the Emperor showed less intensity and less decisiveness in the sunset of his rule. Though he was not the caricature that his critics have presented, age, new pressures and forces have come into play and he was weakened by them.

The Emperor's opponents, particularly the military government that deposed him, portrayed him as an obstacle to progress rather than the progressive individual he was. For a long time, he outmaneuvered, with cunning and daring powerful forces and vested interests in order to introduce changes. His opponents disregard or belittle the many contributions he and his government made for a better Ethiopia. Yet the question remains: to what extent was he an obstacle to change and progress?

I specifically focused on this question in discussions with some of the close former associates of the Emperor. All of them have served their country with distinction and all had some differences with him, be it in their personal or official relationships.

One often outspoken and populist official I had the good fortune to take up this issue with was the late long-time distinguished Foreign

Minister Ketema Yifru. He was among the younger crop that replaced the older veterans of the Ethio-Italian war and the early returnees of students sent abroad. Ato Ketema had held positions at all the levels in the hierarchy of government, starting as a junior official in the Emperor's secretariat. After the fall of the Emperor, Mengistu's military regime imprisoned him for eight years. Our conversations took place in Rome after his release, while he was serving in the World Food Program. Our discussion dealt with his perceptions of the Emperor as a leader and a person. He cited incidents to make the point that the Emperor was very receptive to ideas and often proved to be more progressive than many of his close associates.

While working in the Ministry of the Pen as a middle level official, Ketema's attention was drawn to a draft letter prepared for the signature of the Emperor. The letter detailed the Emperor's intention to divide his lands among his children and grandchildren. Intrigued and somewhat impulsively, he decided to offer his view about the draft to the Emperor. He first sought the concurrence of his immediate and cautious boss to see the Emperor.

"I saw this draft letter prepared for the signature of His Majesty bequeathing his lands to his children and offspring. Do you mind if I take the draft and talk to him about it?" Ketema asked his boss.

The boss was taken aback for a moment but rather coolly said, "No, I do not mind. Go ahead." Aware of the sensitivity of the subject, the boss was in essence saying, "Go ahead. Don't come to me if you are found interfering in something that is above your head."

Ketema took the draft to the Emperor. "Your Majesty, I have brought a draft letter regarding the bequeathing of Your Majesty's land properties. Before signature, may I offer a suggestion?" he said with some confidence, for he had known from previous experience that the Emperor encouraged young officials to express views.

"What is your suggestion? Speak." the Emperor was encouraging, curious as to what Ketema might say about a strictly personal matter.

"Your Majesty, you are giving instructions to give your lands to your children and grandchildren. They already have land and means, and they don't need more. Adding to their wealth will only make them greater targets for criticism. In my view, it will be better to give the land to the tenants who work and live on the land. They need it and they will appreciate the gift much more. And, in the long run, Your Majesty's action will be exemplary and more gratifying."

After he pondered for a while, the Emperor agreed, "You are right. I will not sign this draft. Tell them to prepare another one along the lines you suggest."

Ketema returned to his office and happily conveyed the change of mind to his surprised colleagues and his skeptical boss. He passed the instructions on to the officer assigned asking the latter to apprise him of any further development. Then, one morning, six months later, the junior officer, looking perplexed, reported back to Ketema.

"You remember the letter you asked me to keep an eye on concerning the bequeathing of His Majesty's personal lands. It has been signed as initially drafted," he said, with obvious disappointment. The Emperor had received advice from more influential people who opposed the proposal to give the land to the tenants. After all, if the Emperor gave away his land to the tenants, he would set a precedence that would pressure those who owned significant land property to do the same.

In the late 1950s, a few years before the 1960 attempted coup, the Emperor asked Ketema Yifru what he thought of giving his palace, then known as the Geunete Leul Palace at Yekatit 12 Square, for the establishment of a university, for then Ethiopia had a college, but not a university. Ketema stressed to him that there could not be a better use of the property. So, the Emperor asked him to call three senior officials to his office the following day. He further instructed Ketema to keep the conversation confidential.

As soon as the officials arrived at his office, the Emperor announced that they all would go for a long walk. He then walked his entourage through the Palace grounds, the nearby hospital, the Ministry of Finance, and the grounds of the Prime Minister's office, saying nothing during the entire walk. Back in his office, he informed them that he planned to give his Palace and some of the adjacent properties for the planned university.

He asked for their views that did not take long in coming. The majority opposed the idea; one said that action would be tantamount to "abdication."

Other sources related that the Emperor offered to give the Palace to the university and that he did so after the 1960 coup d'e-tat and the killings of officials in the Palace. One of the senior officials present, according to this source, argued that opponents would contest that the Emperor must have reimbursed himself to give such a generous donation. He contended that the good intentions will be suspect and misconstrued, thus making the gift hardly meaningful.

The two versions differ mainly on when the discussion took place. Ketema's version could have happened indeed before the attempted coup. The second source may have heard of another discussion held after the failure of the coup.

Ketema's perception that the Emperor was forward-looking was so strong that he risked the ire of the Dergue by insisting on this view when they were trying to show otherwise. The Dergue's campaign to portray the Emperor as an obstacle to progress and new ideas was unrelenting, and the Dergue's leadership tried to use long-time associates to discredit him. Ketema narrated how the unscrupulous soldiers tried to get his cooperation to advance their malicious campaign.

"I was taken to the Dergue offices from the place of imprisonment in the basement of the Menelik Palace for questioning," Ketema told me. "A group of officers confronted me with questions that sought confirmation of their biases rather than soliciting honest answers.

"You were one of the close associates of the Emperor. You should know how much of an obstacle he was to new ideas and progress," said the most senior questioner trying to promote a negative assessment.

"I am not going to lie to you and I can only tell you what I know. In all the years that I have worked with the Emperor, I did not find him to be an obstacle to changes and improvement. He was receptive to ideas provided that an idea or an action was explained to him well and with convincing merits. I always found him to be receptive, understanding, and sometimes more forward-looking than most of his officials," he unequivocally told them. Ketema had a lot to lose by such a reply in favor of a fallen ruler. He could have earned goodwill by agreeing with them and giving them the reply that they were after.

Other sources also affirmed Ketema's views. Abebe Kebede's assessment from his long experience of working directly with the Emperor was the same. He confirmed that the Emperor was receptive to and supportive to an idea or proposal, if the concept and the advantages were convincingly explained and argued.

The three "Habte Wold brothers" had a "long hold on government," to the extent that this is possible when real power rested in the hands of the Emperor. The three held various critical ministerial portfolios. The oldest was Ato Makonnen Hapte Wold who was a powerful Minister of Finance and trusted confidant of the Emperor. The second was Ato Akale Work who had served long as Minister of Education, Justice and Ambassador to France. The youngest, Tsahafe Te'ezaz Aklilu, was the longest serving Prime Minister and had also held the post of Minister of Foreign Affairs. He had the further distinction of signing the Charter of the United Nations on behalf of Ethiopia and playing an important role in the federation of Eritrea with Ethiopia. He went furthest in formal education and he was best equipped regarding foreign affairs. He relied greatly on his brother for advice and support concerning the internal social and political matters.

I have known Ato Akale Work very well and Prime Minister Aklilu Habte Wold marginally and mainly in official settings. Prime Minister Aklilu was the chairman of the Board of Trustees for the Trust. I knew Ato Akale Work in official capacity but, since he was married to my aunt, I had the good fortune to know him in less formal settings. He held several portfolios but he was best known as Minister of Education, a capacity in which he played a significant role.

In the diary the Prime Minister's kept while in prison and before his execution gave examples of the Emperor's receptivity to change as well as his vulnerability to pressure. As Prime Minister, Aklilu convinced the Emperor to accept many proposals including land and constitutional reforms, though the Emperor in some instances reversed positions, yielding to conservative and traditionalist advice.

The Prime Minster and the cabinet knew that whatever changes they sought required the Emperor as an ally. The proposal to revise the 1930 Constitution and replace it with a more democratic one encountered a strong opposition, and a draft constitution submitted by a commission was debated extensively. The late Prime Minister confirmed that, subsequent to adoption of the revised constitution, the Emperor accepted the reform of criminal, commercial, and civil laws. Again, after the 1960-attempted coup, the Prime Minister's proposal of governmental reform got full and immediate acceptance.[37]

A general who knew the Emperor closely described a discussion that the Emperor had with his top advisors on the modernization of the armed forces. Conservative elements were urging him to be careful about the creation of a modern army; particularly the establishment of an elite cadet school that they feared could produce individuals bent on revolution. They contended Ethiopia should be able to defend itself, as it did in the past, by mobilizing all its citizens in times of war and conflicts.

The Emperor's position was unequivocal. He told the gathering that such thinking puts self-interest before the needs of the country. He made it clear that a modern and strong army was essential when neighboring countries posed serious threats to the territorial integrity of the country. He assured the gathering that he was prepared to face whatever consequences and pay any price to ensure national security. His commitment paid off and Ethiopia had a small but efficient cadre of officers and well-trained army. This and similar decisions that he approved or even pushed for could, he knew, adversely affect him but benefit the

---

37 Habte Wold, Aklilu. *Historical Diary and Notes* written in Prison. Tobia Vol.2 No.12 1994, pp.19-20.

country.

My experience in the Prize Trust corroborated, albeit in relation to narrower issues, that the Emperor accepted suggestions that were not only new to him but also sometimes went counter to his sentiments. The Trust's Charter had technically excluded him from involvement in the decision of award recipients. His given role was to preside and give the awards at annual ceremonies. This is an unfamiliar role for one who personally approved the hundreds of medal recipients and awards he gave out over the years.

The draft Charter of the Trust had provisions for post-graduate studies abroad but none for scholarships for study locally. A proposal to grant scholarships for study in the university in the country was made but opposed by some of the Trustees and initiators of the idea of the Trust, who feared the proposal could detract from the core mission of the Trust. Despite the opposition, the Emperor's quick acceptance of our proposal led to the creation of a useful scholarship program for study in the national university.

Under the program, those who completed high school with great distinction, about a dozen annually at the time, were automatically given stipends for the four years of study as long as they performed well in their studies. They did not even need to apply. Unlike the awards for study abroad where the sciences were favored, no other conditions were made for the Trust scholarships for study locally. This scholarship scheme was very likely the first privately financed and significant one in the country. It enabled gifted achievers, often from families with no or limited resources, to pursue their studies without financial worry. Recipients proved worthy of recognition for they ended up as a former university president, academicians, and scientists. The current Prime Minister of Ethiopia, Meles Zenawi, was one of the recipients of Prize Trust scholarship for study in the then Haile Selassie I University.[38]

The Trust also initiated a public lecture series, free from elaborate

---

38 Haile Selassie I Memorial Foundation. *Special Issue on 112ᵗʰ Birthday of the Emperor*, July 2004.

formality and structure, for small group of participants. One interesting meeting of scholars on Africa, chaired by the then Executive Secretary of Economic Commission of Africa, Robert E. Gardiner, explored the topic Africa and the World, and its proceedings were published.

His Unfulfilled Wish

The Emperor's positive responses to ideas further encouraged us to propose an event in which the Emperor himself could directly dialogue with a widely representative group of Ethiopian professionals. Many of my age group and younger did not have opportunities to talk informally with him. Accepted or not, the idea was worth trying. At the end of a meeting with him on a different order of business, I asked permission to submit a proposal for his consideration.

"Your Majesty, my peers had no opportunities to hear from you personally of your perceptions and of the problems you encountered as a leader. We would like to ask you questions and hear from Your Majesty directly about the lessons you want to pass on to us, of the things you like, dislikes, the challenges you faced, your assessment of your successes and disappointments. What we know are from books and mostly from the press. We want to dialogue with Your Majesty and hear from Your Majesty directly. I suggest that Your Majesty meet in an informal setting in the Prize Trust with about 120 individuals representative of the various disciplines, professions, and age. The meeting will be small enough to permit dialogue," I said with earnestness. I truly hoped that he would not say no to such an event being held in a foundation that he established and as a part of the public lecture series.

"That is a good idea. We had in the past even offered to teach in the University and share what we know. Give Us the details of your proposal in writing," the Emperor replied enthusiastically. I handed a short memorandum that I had already prepared, hoping he would react favorably.

That same evening, while I was at a meeting in my office, the home phone rang and my wife, Rahel, took the call.

"Is he there?" the elderly voice asked.

"No, he is not. Who is calling?" my wife inquired.

"Where is he at this late hour? Why is he not at home? He should be at his home and should not stay out late. You tell him that," the caller authoritatively asked questions and at the same time gave instructions.

"He is attending a meeting. Who is calling? "Rahel asked again rather uncertain whether or not the caller was a mischievous friend who was trying to remain anonymous. The caller's voice sounded familiar but she could not place it.

"What meetings are held so late? Tell him to call the Palace when he comes home, "the caller finished.

With the mention of the word Palace, my wife immediately recognized that the voice, which had sounded familiar, was that of the Emperor. Very much unnerved by the realization, she had only enough time to say "I will tell him as soon as he comes home," before the Emperor hung up.

When I came home, she excitedly told me that I should call the Palace immediately. She told me of her unsuspecting conversation and the admonition about my coming home late. I was very surprised that he called home. That was the only time he called and what was surprising was that he himself was on the line when my wife answered the phone.

I phoned the Palace and was connected instantly. The operator was obviously expecting my call.

"Where are you spending your evenings? Why do you not hold your meetings early? You should be with your family. We read your memorandum, and We approve your proposal. We will be happy to participate. You go ahead and make the preparations," the Emperor informed me and stayed on the line briefly to hear me say that I will start the preparations immediately.

This was an opportunity even for so few to ask him questions freely and hear his views directly. A list of participants was compiled, and about a month after I got his green light, I asked to see the Emperor to get a decision on a date for the meeting. I preferred to raise the matter directly

with him rather than get the decision through his secretariat. I was concerned that some might advise against the idea.

The audience was granted quickly raising my expectation that the event may after all take place. When I entered his office, I noticed there were three other persons in the room, one of whom was a Trustee. I explained that I asked for an audience to report that the preparations for the meeting were completed and to get an indication of a date for the event.

The Emperor seemed uncomfortable. In a somewhat subdued tone he said, "We had agreed to take part in the discussion meeting that you proposed. But we have been advised against it because some individuals in the group could use the occasion to be problematic."

One of the officials, the Trustee I least expected to be opposed, quickly elaborated, "The idea is very good. But some individuals could ask questions that may be offensive or unacceptable. This will not be good. We should not expose His Majesty to such situations."

I was dumbfound, especially since the speaker was considered very liberal, a man of convictions.

"The persons who will attend are responsible people who are interested in being informed. They are individuals who are genuinely keen to hear from His Majesty his insights and experiences. If necessary, we can submit the questions in advance," I pleaded hoping this approach may be acceptable and alley all fears.

"It will be difficult to control the situation," the same official shot back.

There was silence and I realized that it was already agreed not to go ahead with the event. The Emperor has been persuaded to change his mind, albeit reluctantly. A good opportunity for us and for him was lost because of over-protective advice. In this case and in the case of his offer to lecture at the University, he might have faced some polite but tough questions and made uncomfortable. The Emperor could have successfully held his own and the dialogue could have been mutually beneficial.

Ninety Per Cent Undeveloped

Not very long after I joined the Prize Trust, I was unexpectedly told to come to see the Emperor. I had seen him twice before as the Director of the Trust. It was almost noon when I was hurriedly ushered into his presence. The adjoining waiting room was empty except for a few security officers. I bowed respectfully, if one can call my clumsy bending at the waist as a bow, when I entered his office. Those who know how to bow in front of the monarch showed great skill. Their bows were tantamount, as one foreigner described them, to "the most strenuous pushup." The most skilled individuals, increasingly fewer, in this traditional form of greeting bow so low that their foreheads almost touch the floor. In comparison, my bow could have been viewed as impertinence. My incompetence, like others who have not practiced and mastered this skill, was tolerated as a function of the failings of my generation.

The Emperor's "good morning" sounded warm and welcoming as I entered. He looked relaxed. A member of the Trust's Board was present. The atmosphere signaled to me that the audience was to be uncomplicated. It indeed turned out to be so. I was called to receive two publications that dealt with his early travels for the small library in the Trust.

"We think these two publications will be useful to the Trust library. We will be happy to donate more books whenever we identify those that might be of use. We have encouraged others to do the same," he said while handing me the publications. He expressed his wish that the library becomes a repository of select books.

I confirmed that was the intention, profusely thanked him, and waited for the signal to be excused. Instead of dismissing me, he turned aside and looked out of the window. For a minute or so, he seemed lost in thought and did not say anything. He was looking out through his window at the largely rusted corrugated iron rooftops of old buildings visible from his office. He finally broke the silence, almost talking to himself, and still looking out of the window, he said, "You realize that Ethiopia is not

developed even ten percent of its potentials. Not even ten per cent," he repeated.

I was astonished to hear such a critical remark of his rule. He turned and looked at us after he made that remark. I was at a loss as to how to react. I could not say that he was right because that would have been indirectly criticizing his rule. Nor could I disagree because what he said was correct. I kept silent. The other person present seemed less surprised. It was perhaps not the first time that he had heard such an observation. He commented, "It was through Your Majesty's efforts that Ethiopia has come so far."

"Even if that were true, a lot has yet to be done. A lot has yet to be done," the Emperor continued, in a sincere expression of dissatisfaction.

When I later told some of my friends of his remarks, their reactions were mixed. The cynics contended that he made the comments only to hear what we had to say. They surmised that the official must have quickly read the Emperor's intention and cleverly made the flattering remark. Others said that the Emperor meant what he said and he had on other occasions expressed even stronger frustrations and harsher sentiments on the tempo of the nation's progress

Six fellow graduates who were received by the Emperor before their departure for graduate studies abroad were told of a similar assessment of Ethiopia's stage of development. In response to a statement by the spokesman of the group, the Emperor wished them success in their studies and implored, as he always did on such occasions, that upon their return they diligently serve their "poor country" and help bring about her speedy development. Interestingly, the group noticed with surprise that the press had left out the word "poor" in a sanitized article covering the group's audience with the Emperor.

The Emperor's remark on the country's progress did not seem insincere fishing for compliments. Besides, our praise or condemnation would have had no significance. He received praise and flattery daily. More importantly, he, a man who has faced and lived with Ethiopia's development challenges and visited so many developed countries, could not but believe that Ethiopia's huge development work was in the future.

Larger Focus

The Emperor treasured Ethiopia's rich cultures and values and believed strongly that they should not be violated by the imposition of hasty and superficial external values. His conviction about the richness of Ethiopian culture and learning was so strong that he considered the well-known centers of learning such as those in Gondar as comparable to institutions offering the theological and philosophical learning in Europe. He twice challenged us to show him why the traditional scholars who taught *"qene and zema"* were not intellectually comparable to the professors around in the universities. He was thinking about *'liqnet'*, to be a learned person.

He welcomed new knowledge and technology but argued that its acquisition be founded in harmony with the country's own heritage. He pressured, cajoled, and urged youth to know and be proud of and appreciative of the true worth of their country's unique history, the cultures, and values, and institutions. This commitment to the Ethiopian heritage as a basis for development was often reflected in his pronouncements and speeches. His deep concern with ensuring change founded on heritage and values was, some argue, a factor for the slow tempo of change, particularly political. Any fears he may have had did not prevent him from slowly pursuing reforms and introducing new services. He may have underestimated the growing need to speed up change. The imponderable constraints of limited funds, and the underdeveloped infrastructure etc., no doubt contributed to the slow pace of economic transformation. Nor were loans, grants and aid available any where near the level needed.

The Emperor focused on national needs, especially in motivating young people. At every encounter with young people, as a group or individually, he drove home the importance of duty and service to the country. This unrelenting emphasis on service paid dividends in that most graduates of the fifties and sixties hurried home to "serve their country" immediately after completion of their studies abroad. And they did serve well.

Emperor opening an art and book exhibition organized by the National Commission of Unesco, 1972. Chairman of Commission and Minister of Education, Ato Seifu Maheteme Selassie at the left of the Emperor.

He believed this commitment to service to the country was vital to the future of the Ethiopia's development and to transcend narrow ethnic or regional attachments. He succeeded to a remarkable degree for there is no better testimony to this success than the fact that, Ethiopian identity rather than any ethnic identity, came first to the minds of most Ethiopians – even after ethnicity became an issue in the post-Haile Selassie era. Most people in my generation made light of and teased each other about being of this or that ethnic group with many jokes, nicknames, and stories to go around about each ethnic group. Friendships were based on individual chemistry and these friendships continued throughout life. I cherish the fact that my group of six close friends consisted of an Oromo, a Gurage, an Adere, and Amhara.

It was the sense of collective identity rather than an ironclad rule that kept Ethiopia united and relatively stable for so long under Haile Selassie. The Emperor had Teodros' zeal and passion for a united Ethiopia, Menelik's commitment to change and modernization, and Yohanese's faith-based and flexible attitude to political foes and malcontents.

It is not surprising that, these facts not withstanding, many of his strongest critics even from among those who were his associates seem to harbor hidden anger arising out of ethnic and regional loyalty and/ or unfulfilled ambitions. Most of the leaders of the student movements that went into exile or underground were the exceptions. The student movement and opposition leaders for the most part, not exclusively, dealt with national issues and ideological biases that mostly reflected the global pro-socialism wave among youth at the time. Even among these, there were however those who led 'liberation movements' that were motivated by regional and ethnic loyalties. Leaders in the Tigray People Liberation Front (TPLF) and Eritrean People Liberation Front (EPLF) ultimately came out to pursue their hidden agenda, an agenda that reflected tribal and ethnic rivalries and claims.

Some of the Emperor's critics have also contended, at times with vindictiveness, that he favored the Amhara and perpetuated an Amhara rule. Many conveniently ignore that the Emperor had Amhara,

Oromo, Gurage and Tigrean blood and his sons and daughters were married to individuals of Oromo, Gurage, and Tigrean parentage. Many demonize him and Emperor Menelik to vent their anti-Amhara feelings and, and anti-Shewa feelings in some quarters, and promote their personal, regional, and ethnic interests. This self-serving charge has to be considered from at least two respects. Has he relied on the Amhara as his power base? Has he benefited the Amhara to the detriment of other ethnic groups by siphoning resources and favoring development efforts in Shewa, Gondar, Gojam and Wollo where the Amhara constitute dominant or significant ethnic groups?

The support from the Amhara was critically important because no leader could assume and stay in power, as it was shown many times, without the support of the large Amhara population. The same is true of the need for support of the large Oromo population. The Emperor counted on, even took for granted, as did his predecessors, the Amhara support. At the same time, the key players in efforts to prevent him from coming to power and, later, to topple him were Amhara.

His "Amhara" government included personalities from the Oromo, Tigray, Eritrea, Wolaita and Gurage etc. in the armed forces, provincial administration, in the civil service, in the cabinet. Tigreans, Oromo, Gurage prominently figured among the most known and senior generals. As the number of the educated grew, recruitment to services and government was in the main based on merit and training. Qualifications of professionals rather than their ethnic origin were by and large the main criteria for positions. Ethnic bias or use of "connections" did exist but they played a decreasing and not a determining role for employment and upward mobility for the majority of the educated.

As regards the contention that he favored the Amhara regions, the developmental status of Shewa, Gondar and Gojam are monumental testimonies that Haile Selassie's rule did not give greater priority to these regions where infrastructure, services were still comparatively minimal. Even historic and scenic places such as close by Ankober had hardly any hotel or health services and amenities. Had Haile Selassie's government diverted substantial resources to these regions, the potentials of the Amhara dominated regions would have been significantly realized.

It is ironic that those who accused the Emperor and his government of ethnic bias turned out to be ardent advocates of ethnicity and even going to the extreme of making ethnicity government policy.

The effort to fight underdevelopment faced by the Haile Selassie government was complicated by the urgent need to safeguard other broader national interests. It had to try to keep Eritrea as an integral part of Ethiopia and sustain the overall unity of the country. Ethiopia constantly faced real threats from Arab countries, which sought to benefit from the destabilization of what they perceived as a Christian-dominated Ethiopia. In the East, the threats from Somalia forced allocations of meager resources to sustain a significant military presence. These priority challenges, rather than a deliberate policy of suppression of ethnic groups, as some feel, consumed a good portion of the limited resources available and contributed to slow overall development work.

Despite the claims that impoverished Ethiopia benefited from the annexation of Eritrea, the resource flow to Eritrea was a heavy burden on the country's treasury. Special treatment was given, albeit for national political gains, to Eritrea by the Emperor and the government in their efforts to please the population and subvert the foreign-backed guerrilla movement. Eritrea got better relative share of national resources than the supposedly favored regions. If one takes education, schools were concentrated in densely populated locations such as towns in the country as a whole. "Fifty eight per cent of the total enrollment in senior secondary schools in 1970-1971 was in cosmopolitan Addis Ababa, Shewa, and Eritrea which had only about 27 % of its secondary school-age population. At the other end of the scale, five provinces had only one secondary school each with enrollments in each averaging only a little more than 800."[39] Schools in Eritrea were started in areas heretofore neglected. An existing school was upgraded to a university in Asmara and Eritreans constituted a significant presence in higher institutions in Addis Ababa and elsewhere in the country. In the business sector, nothing is more telling than the fact that a good proportion expelled by the EPRDF government were wealthy Eritreans who had prospered by living and working in all the regions of Ethiopia.

The Emperor had, as Hans Wilhelm Lockot points out, a basic vision or 'mission' for Ethiopia and a commitment that did not waiver, even under the most trying circumstances. He saw Ethiopia as a nation with historic obligations and destiny and a country that must remain united, whatever the cost. He pursued the advancement and reinforcement of this vision with all available means. He used with remarkable success the institutions of the monarchy and the church, the schools, inclusion and inter-marriage, money and appointments, the gloved fist and house arrests, intimidation and incentives. He resorted to violence and force sparingly and often with reluctance. In his last days, he even reportedly refused to use force to counter the impending military takeover despite the pleas and pressure of some of his supporters to let them fight it out.

The Emperor ruled more with skill, deals, and intimidation rather than the use of force, though he did not hesitate to use it when necessary. He controlled adversaries with a mixture of threat and leniency, some times scored points by doing nothing at all when he had grounds to be tough or punitive.

Ato Tekle Tsadik Mekuria, the respected writer and once ambassador and cabinet minister, sided with those who attempted the overthrow of the Emperor in 1960. He told me of his case with amusement and to some extent lingering puzzlement. At the time, he headed the Ethiopian mission in Israel, and he and his colleagues had champagne flowing, prematurely celebrating the ouster of the Emperor. Tekle Tsadik even tried unsuccessfully to see the head of his host government to lobby

---

39 Report Of The Education Sector Review: *Education: Challenge To The Nation*, Addis Ababa, 1972, II-8.

for support for the coup. The host government wisely took a cautious attitude and declined the request.

The attempted coup collapsed quickly, and many of the coup leaders were arrested. Tekle Tsadik waited to hear of repercussions regarding his own future. Nothing happened. He continued in his job for a while, puzzled by the silence. He finally decided to request permission to go to France, ostensibly to get medical treatment. In fact, he planned to relocate there and seek political asylum. Though he expected a recall or some unfavorable reaction, his request to go to Paris was approved.

From Paris, he felt confident enough to write to the Emperor, stressing the importance of conducting a fair trial for the coup participants. Tekle Tsadik stressed that the international community was closely watching events in Ethiopia. The Emperor replied, thanking him for his views and assuring him that it will be up to the courts to decide on their fate.

There was no mention of his support to the failed coup in the letter. Instead, he was soon after appointed ambassador to a new duty station. His support to the attempted coup never came up, and he went on to serve in other senior positions. Tekle Tsadik never found out if the Emperor deliberately ignored his action or he simply did know about it. He suspected that the Emperor heard of the incident and the premature champagne celebration. After all, the ambassador's short-lived shift in alliance was covered in the media of his host country. Since the host government was also supportive of the Emperor, it is difficult to believe that it did not somehow inform the Emperor or his officials.

Others accused of conspiring against the Emperor were pardoned and even appointed to high posts. He was generally forgiving "as long as the offender asked for forgiveness." He was criticized for rehabilitating and appointing some, who had allegedly collaborated with Italy, favored the cessation of Eritrea, or suspected of secretly supporting the Eritrean cause. Several officials who eventually came out public in their support to the Eritrean independence were known to the government but remained untouched. It was deemed better to have them in the government and keep an eye on them. A senior official told me that the government knew those who from within the government were actively supporting the Eritrean session efforts. He even mentioned two friends of mine. I did not believe him, until much later when they joined the Eritrean government.

There are also those who attest that "the Emperor was harsh and punitive" in those cases where his grudge or displeasure was very strong. He was known to have held grudges too long against some who offended him, and even against their children. A friend sadly told me of a judge who for over thirty years lived under house arrest with minimal financial support. The individual who claimed innocence refused to apologize and seek pardon.

The Emperor worked hard and was able to influence the vast majority of the Ethiopian people that the country was one and indivisible and their prosperity and future depended on this common foundation. Without it, hostile neighbors and expansionists would endanger unity and territorial integrity. The Emperor made all segments of the society believe that commitment to the indivisibility of Ethiopia and to die for it was a given. The army, air force, the militia, and the navy made up an Ethiopian armed force that fought with pride and commitment along the Somali front and Eritrea did so for this national cause.

Even some of the leaders of the EPRDF government, who started with the defamation of the national flag and questioned the very reality of the Ethiopian State, have back-pedaled when faced with the undying commitment of the people to the Ethiopian identity, an identity that has been promoted and nurtured in so many ways by preceding rulers and governments. It was in the end by capitalizing on this commitment that the present government rallied the people to fight the recent Eritrean incursions. The youth of Ethiopia from all ethnic groups have responded with patriotism to defend "their flag and Ethiopia." The government interestingly launched a National Flag Day in 2008.

There is no greater tribute to Emperor Haile Selassie than this defense, even by his opponents, of his basic mission: to preserve a united multi-ethnic country. Ethiopians from all walks of life, ethnic and religious background, are fighting to uphold and sustain this commitment.

9

A Great Life Indeed

In August 1972, Ato Akale Work Habte Wold, the then Minster of Justice and General Assefa Ayana, Commander of the Imperial Air Force, were traveling to Paris. I, with my wife Rahel, our sons Dereje and Dehne, was on the same flight on the way to join the United Nations Development Programme in New York with a stop over for a night in Paris. The minister and the general had gone there on official business. Ato Akale Work invited us for breakfast the next day before we left for New York. He enjoyed the hour chatting and playing with our little boys who were three and five. As we said good-bye, he took me to the side and, in a fatherly way, gave me advice about the future.

"You have to think about your family from now on. Stay in the United Nations where you want to work and educate your children. As far as we are concerned in Ethiopia, it is finished," he sadly remarked and we parted. Little did I suspect that would be the last time we talked to this patriotic Ethiopian and distinguished public servant. He was one of the sixty officials who were savagely and without trial executed by the Dergue two years later on November 23, 1974.

My father who was a member of the upper house of Parliament and who was abreast of the local political winds, gave me the same fatalistic warning when I said good-bye to him a day earlier, at the airport in Addis Ababa.

"I initially did not like the idea of your leaving. But when I think about the future, it is the right thing to do. You and your family will survive to tell about us," he gloomily said.

"You should not think so negatively about the future. As far as I am concerned, I am going only for two years. My contract is for two years," I replied because this was indeed the case.

"No, you continue there. Those of you who will be outside the country will at least be spared the consequences of the conflicts that will surely come, and may be destroy us all. And soon!" he ended as he said good-bye.

A sense of foreboding was widespread among government officials and civil servants. Yet, even as people expected uneasy change and turbulence, few anticipated the disaster that engulfed the country when change came. Who else but officials who believed that there would be reasonable order and justice in change would walk into military barracks and voluntarily surrender or stay at home instead of fleeing? These officials and others rounded up were brutally and without a modicum of justice executed. This barbaric act by the Dergue started the dark days Ethiopians had to go through under the Mengistu military regime.

In hindsight, it is puzzling that the government and the more informed citizenry, which saw turbulence coming, could not find ways to avert or manage it. Equally tragic is the opportunity missed by the succeeding government to make the necessary changes peacefully and build on the positive achievements of the Emperor and his associates.

Regardless, the Emperor's achievements and his place in history need to be seen within the context of his time, the forces he had to contend with, his personal limitations and strengths, and vision. All-too-often, the evaluation of his successes and failures has been influenced by ideological biases, ethnic affiliations, and personal feelings that have clouded the evaluation of his contributions and of him as a person and leader.

As the most recent monarch whose rule was known first-hand to most people, it is understandable that the Emperor comes under greater scrutiny than his predecessors. But the relentless effort to discredit him sometimes went to ludicrous extremes. Some have claimed that whatever he did was only for personal glory and edification. For example, a delegation from the Dergue regime was in New York for the annual United Nations General Assembly meeting in the late seventies. The then foreign minister addressed an Ethiopian gathering at a dinner hosted by the Ethiopian Permanent Representative to the United Nations. For the most part, the Minister focused on the "progress" made since the military takeover. He described how much better off people were after the sweeping nationalization of land, houses, and other drastic changes by the military regime. Presumably to show objectivity, he at one point grudgingly credited the former "Negus" with important achievements in foreign relations, citing the Emperor's role in the establishment of the Organization of African Unity, the location of the United Nations Economic Commission Secretariat in Addis Ababa, and the recognition Ethiopia had attained internationally. While these praiseful words were flowing, he noticed that his senior military deputy sitting next to him was casting disapproving glances his way. The glances soon changed to frowns, if not to a threatening stare. The minister realized that he has trespassed into a forbidden zone, and he quickly reversed gears. He retreated to the usual allegation that "of course, what he (the Negus) did internationally was for selfish reasons and to enhance his ego and fame!"

The minister had to keep in line with the regime's biased campaign of discrediting the Emperor. After the meeting broke up, many of the guests expressed amazement by the lack of objectivity, and commented that, even if it were true that the Emperor had an insatiable thirst for glory, Ethiopians should ignore it and enjoy the international stature and benefits the Emperor and his government brought to the country.

His Share of Shortcomings

The Emperor had his share of shortcomings. It would have been surprising if he did not have some of the traits often manifested by political leaders. Some associates have cited "overarching" ambition, thirst for power, a penchant for wheeling and dealing, and a degree of selfishness. Biographies on great leaders such as Sir Winston Churchill, President John F. Kennedy, Dr. Kwame Nkrumah, to mention a few, reveal in these leaders some of such traits, and others less complimentary. But the weaknesses are ignored or outweighed by their great achievements and the leadership they provided for their countries.

Yet two weaknesses became more pronounced and affected the Emperor's performance and well-known self-confidence as he approached the sunset of his life. The first and often cited weakness was his failure to stand firm on positions that he had taken because of others' counsel, distorted information, and his efforts to appease. His initial reactions and instinctive response to convincing proposals or ideas were often positive and progressive. Unfortunately he reversed many of them, often reluctantly, when other forces intervened and presented opposing arguments, ostensibly to safeguard his interest or that of the state. Many of his ministers and senior officials felt frustrated because they were forced to spend significant time trying to adapt to changed positions or to have earlier decisions reinstated. The consequences of this weakness, especially when there was so much decision-making power in his hands, were far-reaching in many critical affairs of state.

The Prime Minister had complained in public inquiry hearings, after the military took over, that the Emperor frequently reversed decisions they had agreed on and he approved because of interferences. He and ministers often complained that they spent precious time "defending their turf" and fighting spoilers. The Prime Minister's conversation with Ato Teshome Gebre Mariam Bokan in prison, not long before the Prime Minister, along with other senior officials was executed, sheds further light on the way the Emperor yielded to interventions and appeals from individuals and pressure groups.

This weakness was manifest at the critical juncture when Aklilu Hapte Wold's cabinet resigned and the Emperor had to replace it.

The Emperor reportedly picked Lt. General Abiy Abebe first as a replacement. Then, as the General was preparing his acceptance speech, the Emperor yielded to pressure and appointed Ledj Endalkachew Makonnen instead. How the Emperor ended up with this decision was a subject of rumor and speculation. One version was Endalkachew's supporters told the Emperor that, although this was not the case, the armed forces wanted the younger and educated Endalkachew as Prime Minister. Endalkachew's qualifications were not the issue. Such vacillation at a time of crisis was inviting confusion.

Substantively and symbolically important decisions were reversed or delayed when advisers pointed out possible negative consequences. While a leader may have to change his mind to balance contending forces, it is counterproductive to do so if it affects the exercise of delegated power or reform efforts. It is difficult to know if the Emperor fully recognized this weakness for the serious shortcoming it was.

The Emperor showed this disposition to accept derailing advice, even in situations over which he had complete control. Some of the Prize Trust incidents discussed in this book highlight this problem. Just before the charter of the Prize Trust was issued, an influential individual put the suggestion that a language academy rather than a prize trust be established. The Emperor considered, though he did not endorse, this suggestion. Not only was the timing for the proposal well after measures had been taken to publicize the establishment of the Trust, the idea did not also have significant support, except among a few such as linguists and writers.

He accepted the suggestion that he should give his private lands to the people working on it. He enthusiastically agreed to meet with a cross section of intellectuals and professionals to freely and directly dialogue with them on his rule, development of the country etc. His wish to give his former palace to the university before the 1960 attempted coup d'état was delayed due to contrary advice. The Emperor's desire to lecture in the University was not realized thanks to those who excessively overprotected him. Although he had complete say and he was initially positively disposed in all these cases, he gave in to contrary counsel, backtracked or hesitated.

Some confidants also exerted influence well beyond the powers or relevance of the offices they held. A minor but illustrative example was a case when an official claimed some land that would have given him virtual control of a small water canal that irrigated Prize Trust properties. Even a committee of senior officials, designated by the Emperor to look into the contending claims of the individual and the Trust, failed to resolve the dispute.[40] The Board of Trustees was clearly uncomfortable to take up the issue at all, but, in the end, the Board decided that the Trust should not yield to the demand. After the Board meeting ended and we were all leaving the room when the chairman, the Prime Minister, asked me to stay behind. "Please do not bring issues that involve this individual to our meeting. You find solutions. It is very important," he said, half requesting, and half instructing. The message was clear. He needed the goodwill of the individual to do his work, and he could not antagonize him. The individual had such "sway" with the Emperor that even the Prime Minister had to seek the individual's alliance.

The Emperor's susceptibility to pressure and tendency to change his mind because of contrary advice, good and bad, raises the question of whether he was as all-powerful as many claimed. He was often described as one with absolute power, and he indeed had power. Yet the Emperor allowed others to advise him or to have a strong influence over him in the exercise of his power. Ayalew Wolde Giorgis justifiably assesses that "Haile Selassie was never a tyrant or an absolute monarch."[41]

The Emperor's second shortcoming was the feeling of

---

40 The group went to the farm and reviewed the case. My colleagues and I were unable to present a critical document that disappeared from the office files on the eve of the committee's mission. The document reappeared when it was put back in the filing cabinet where it was always located._

41 Wolde Giorgis, Ayalew. *In the Palace of Emperor Haile Selassie*, Southern Heritage Press, USA, 2002 p. XI.

indispensability both on his part, in the view of his associates, and the public. Some contend that he was indispensable throughout his life. For decades, especially when the educated manpower was hardly existent and when his reformist and enlightened efforts were far ahead of most of his contemporaries, he was, indeed, indispensable. On his part, this feeling was also founded on his sense of 'mission' and destiny as well as his direct daily involvement in the daily business of the country. He embraced, as did his predecessors, the notion that the Almighty had chosen him to govern and serve the historical land of Ethiopia. A deeply religious man, he believed God played a role in what he did and did not mind the perpetuation of the belief that he was anointed as "Elect of God."

The Ethiopian Orthodox Tewahedo Church endorsed the claim to this divine call. Because of this belief, the church had support through the person of the monarch at the very center of power, and the monarchs had in reciprocity the indispensable backing of the powerful institution of the church that above forty per cent of the population followed. They needed each other even though the Emperor increasingly reduced the involvement of the church in state matters.

The belief that he had his roots in the Solomonic dynasty and was referred to as the Lion of Judah were part of the lore. Leaders and countries have their heroes and heroic feats, legends and myths to legitimize their claim to rule and to forge and perpetuate a collective identity. Ethiopia and Emperor Haile Selassie had theirs in the claim to kinship to King Solomon and divine selection.

References to him as "the Elect of God," and The Lion of Judah" were hardly mentioned in the latter part of his reign. These designations had become out of tune with the times, but they had served both historical and political purposes.

They were not publicly discarded but quietly abandoned. Still, the above-mentioned convictions and the decades of media accolades at home and abroad further nurtured in him the feeling of centrality and indispensability.

Officials and the public were uncertain of what would follow when he was no more on the scene. His supporters and officials saw him as the individual who had the general acceptance and track record to hold the country together. Their perception was not simply a function of their loyalty to him, as some writers have contended. There were, for instance, many supporters and opponents who would have liked to see him retain a symbolic, honorary role, – even as they wanted him removed from the political center.

A revealing conversation on this subject with an influential minister illustrates the dilemma that many faced. The minister was most knowledgeable about and adept in domestic politics. Our conversation took place in the late sixties when university students were demonstrating and calling for land and political reforms. I had sparingly discussed politics with the minister, though I had known him well enough to feel free to do so. Yet the student demands, which had broad sympathy, could not but become a subject of conversation. As one of the officers of the University Alumni Association at the time, the demands of the students and the strikes were understandably of particular interest to my colleagues and me. The officers of the University Alumni Association were, at times, involved in mediation between the university administration, the government and the students.[42] The demands of the strike had broad implications to basic reforms and the continued role of the Emperor and the government structure.

"I note that you are critical and unhappy with the current national situation and the performance of the government of which you are not only a part but also a very important part. The students, you and other

---

42 The mediation effort sometimes put the Alumni Association in difficulties. The student activists added drama to their strike by taking over a small coffee shop run by the Alumni Association. This action precipitated a mini crisis. The Association owned only the business while the house belonged to the University. Our Association had to either surrender to the forceful seizure by the students or to take the matter to court. We avoided being caught in the middle between the government and the students by simply selling the business for 500 birr to the students. We neither technically yielded to forceful seizure nor did we become the cause and justification for strong government action against the students who would have lost in court.

government officials—we are all critical. You and the ministers are expected to bring about the necessary changes. Don't you think there is urgency? Don't you think that, if nothing is done to bring about real changes, either the military or some extremely radical group could take over?" I asked the minister, following his critical remarks about the situation.

"Yes we are not happy with the pace of change and development despite the many good and important things the government is doing and in spite of so many difficulties, especially the lack of resources. In regards to basic changes, the Prime Minister cannot do anything without the involvement of the Emperor. He cannot even spend his own office budget without arousing some suspicion and scrutiny. About the future, you surely don't think we do not know that the military could very likely take over. That is a real possibility.

Like all of you, we know the Emperor is advancing in age and losing ground. If he is removed without a strong and uniting successor, the chaos that we all fear will engulf the country. I assure you that it will be easy to remove him. The real problem is who will replace him. I am convinced that, if he is removed without a good successor, we will devour each other!"

So I asked, "If you cannot make substantive reforms, why don't the Prime Minister and the cabinet resign?"

"The Emperor would not, in the first place, give us release. More important, we have to do what we can for the country. We have no choice but to go on. In any case, we cannot hand over the country to very conservative elements." Other senior ministers had shared similar convictions and often expressed them privately.

The Emperor's belief in his indispensability more than self-centered autocracy could be the main reason that the Emperor was reluctant to hand over or share more power with his designated successor and Parliament. This perception of himself, albeit concern with the possibility of being sidelined as well, appear to have made him resistant to suggestions for accelerated institutionalization of the political process and to the adoption of practices that could facilitate his gradual phasing out. Some of his staunchest supporters urged him to make substantive changes in this direction. Ketema Yifru, who admired the Emperor, did so in writing urging the Emperor to delegate power to the Crown Prince Asfaw Wossen and the people.[43] Other close associates had advised him to move towards a stronger parliament, to revise the constitution, to delegate more power to the prime minister and cabinet, and to assume an elder statesman role.[44]

The Emperor procrastinated. The public, especially the educated, anticipated that he would retire or delegate power and phase out. Dr. Adam Abdallah, a friend who gives due credit to the Emperor's achievements, best reflected the view of many when he commented:

"I was greatly disappointed and let down when he failed to retire at his eightieth birthday. Had he done so, my great admiration for him would have lasted as long as I live. But he hung on too long as a result of which the chaotic change of power and turmoil followed."

There were, no doubt, many who advised caution about the suggested reforms. These people underestimated or ignored, the fact that the profile of Ethiopia and the people had greatly changed. The armed forces, for instance, were staffed with younger people with higher level of education than was the case in the fifties and early sixties. Students were not only active but also better united around specific issues. The country had entered a new era where the demands for change and for the decrease of his centrality had increased.

Ayalew Wolde Giorgis encapsules the consequences of indispensability or centrality thus:

> "The problem with Haile Selassie's type of leadership is
> that it cannot survive without the central individual. When
> His Majesty departed from the scene in a horrifying and

---

43 Ketema Yifru's letter, July 1971 (Nehasse 6, 1963), Short Life History issued at Memoriam, July 1994.

44 Memorandum by five close associates published in the Reporter, April 7, 2003.

catastrophic manner, so did all the history and lofty ideals
for which he stood as a shining example."[45]

One also wonders about how much the ambivalence of his senior
colleagues played a role in the undoing of the Emperor's rule. The
able, sophisticated and often accomplished individuals in the cabinet
and armed forces were torn between loyalty to, and respect for,
the Emperor and the recognition that he needed to play a reduced
role. The Emperor was the fatherly figure who "mentored" them; he
facilitated their education. He appointed and advanced them in their
careers. The Ethiopian respect for age and father figures in general,
as well as the many admirable achievements of the Emperor weighed
heavily on their consciences. Even those who organized serious *coup*
attempts did not want violence or to take his life.

Although there were ample opportunities, there were hardly any
serious attempts to remove him by taking his life. General Mengistu
Neway and Ato Germame Neway staged their attempt while he was
abroad. Colonel Mengistu Haile Mariam even claimed that he had
nothing to do with the Emperor's death, which he attributed to illness.
According to Mengistu Haile Mariam, the Dergue leadership did not
plan or demand the execution of the Emperor's associates either. He
claimed a larger military committee (600 strong) called to decide on
the fate of the then head of state, General Aman Andom, bulldozed the
decision to execute the senior officials.[46] His claim notwithstanding,it
is widely believed that Colonel Mengistu Haile Mariam ordered his
close associates to kill the Emperor and secretely and unceremoniously
bury him.

---

45 Wolde Giorgis, Ayalew W. *In the Palace of Emperor Haile Selassie*, Southern Heritage Press,
2002, p.189.

46 Anbese, Genet Ayele, *Recollection of Colonel Mengistu Haile Maryam*, Mega Publishing 23
Press, Addis Ababa, pp.165-169.

* Berihun Kebede's The History of Atse Haile Selassie provides detailed statistics and
information on specific accomplishments of the Haile Selassie's years.

Enduring Contributions

The Emperor's leadership and contributions were undeniably the reason for the relative peace and national unity that prevailed during the nearly half century. Whatever his shortcomings, he was a singularly able leader who gave Ethiopians a sense of pride in their unity, history and rich cultures and earned the nation respected status in the international arena. He and his patriotic and dedicated colleagues laid a firm foundation and introduced many changes and services. The change to a strong central government, the establishment of the airlines, telecommunications, the air force and military, the introduction of a new constitution with the move towards parliamentary rule, the expansion and improvement of the school system, roads, electric power, highways and Ethiopia's active and respected membership in the international community stand and remain witness to his work and the good contributions of those who served with him.

He saw the need of educating the people politically through slow constitutional change. He pushed for the harmonization of change with culture and tradition, and the promotion of *Ethiopianness*. Underlying all the educational effort, development work and accomplishment was the successful effort to develop quality manpower, albeit small, through the academic as well as specialized professional training institutions.

Haile Selassie's Government educated the young at home and abroad; it put the successful ones in responsible positions irrespective of ethnic background and origin. It accelerated, at times to the chagrin of donors and international institutions, the replacement of expatriate managers by nationals. The airlines, telecommunications, the air force and army, institutions of learning, hospitals, electric and highway authorities were among the many services and institutions and enterprises where trained nationals took over and performed with success and dedication. The University and colleges, which were run and staffed by high-caliber nationals at all levels, were the best example of Ethiopianization in quality and reach.

Graduates from the professional and specialized schools such as the commercial school, the air force, and technical schools also joined private business and eventually replaced expatriate managers and took over established firms and companies. The control by trained nationals of top and middle-level positions or as experts became the norm in the late fifties and sixties.

So much of the considerable capacity built up through careful nurturing and at great cost to the country has been regrettably lost to others through brain drain because of the turbulence and selfish political ends of succeeding governments. Later governments' shortsighted policies and paranoia resulted in the exile of thousands of trained and experienced nationals, as well as the non-utilization of significant trained and experienced manpower that remained in the country. Who but those with shortsighted political aims would demobilize en masse career soldiers and dismiss professionals in the civil service on the basis of ethnic considerations and waste the investment in human resources?

The return of most in the Diaspora is unlikely when their country's history, collective identity, and traditional harmonious co-existence are buffeted by divisive ethnic policies, lack of adequate incentives, and a threatening political climate. Many Ethiopians will return or invest substantially in their home country when a truly democratic system of government provides them, more than anything, with a sense of security and peace in their country and the sub-region. Some recent actions by the government, such as flexibility in visa requirements, in investment policies, and in making land more easily available for home building, are positive steps but cannot substitute for the need for a climate free of uncertainty and insecurity. The practice of changing policies and legal statutes to suit the whims and interests of the ruling regime, as witnessed during and after the May 2005 national election, also casts serious doubts in the minds of potential investors.

The loss of human capital in the last decades have not been only due to brain drain. Internal displacement and catastrophic loss of life occurred due to turbulence and conflicts that might have been minimized, if not averted, by more patient, diplomatic initiatives and efforts. Tension and fear of further conflicts with Eritrea are still of continuing concern not only to the two countries but the international community as well. Many Ethiopians remain angry not only by Eritrea's cessation but by the way that it came about. The Ethiopian people, except those of Eritrean descent, had no say in the decision; the government in power unashamedly nurtured and supported cessation. None of the reasons it gave, especially the right of cessation, would have appealed, had there been a national referendum, to the fiercely nationalistic majority of the Ethiopian people.

The government of Prime Minister Meles Zenawi rendered futile the years of sacrifice of lives and resources that Ethiopia put in the conflict in Eritrea. Despite the claim that Ethiopia can do without her traditional ports, it committed a grave and harmful mistake of rendering Ethiopia landlocked and sowing the seeds for continued conflict between Ethiopians and Eritreans. A return to a federal status for Eritrea was, many believe, an option in post-Haile Selassie era and one that could have ensured peace and mutually beneficial development. The Emperor first secured the federation of Eritrea with Ethiopia and then integrated it fully as part of Ethiopia following a plebiscite. When the Eritrean independence movement gathered momentum, it became politically harder for him and the government to revert to a federal arrangement in Eritrea. A government that united Eritrea with Ethiopia could not have, although desirable, easily turned around and agreed to federation much less to cessation of an important part of the country. It is also doubtful if most of the leadership in the Haile Selassie government believed that the Eritrean situation was so desperate to force a compromise.

The Dergue and the current government had the federation option, which might have appealed to both sides. This was the least that could have been pursued if Ethiopia's interests, such as access to the sea, were to be protected. Although they could have at the least and as a last resort let Eritrea break away on its own, Prime Minister Meles Zenawi and his supporters did the " unthinkable to Ethiopians" at large and promoted Eritrea's breakaway in the United Nations. This act and the creation of regional states on ethnic and language lines have ensured the Prime Minister and his government a controversial, if not a dubious, place in Ethiopia's contemporary history. The EPRDF undervalues the fact that decentralization, delegation of authority to administrative regions, as well as ensuring equality and accommodation of cultural and language differences could be the better and tested alternative than the establishment of ethnic-based regions and management with its potential dangers to Ethiopia's unity. Let us hope that the EPRDF has not, because of its experimental ethnic–based policies, placed Ethiopia on the edge of a precipice, even perched it on an explosive powder keg. The signs of ethnic and tribal tensions are already showing and narrowly focused ethnic and tribal groups attack the Ethiopianness delicately cultivated over the years. The solace and hope for the Ethiopian people lies however in the fact that the Ethiopian entity and Ethiopianness will endure, not only because of the widely shared strong nationalistic feeling, but because it is in the interest of all economically, politically, and in sustaining sub-regional peace.

Ethiopia's unity and territorial integrity has been preserved through skillful diplomacy, elite armed forces, a credible Ethiopian image and international status. Ethiopia's role beginning with the Emperor's globally famous address at the League of Nations, her founding member status in the United Nations, participation with elite UN forces in Korea and the Congo, leadership in the establishment of the OAU, the mediation efforts in African conflicts were all commendable achievements and a result of refined diplomacy. Ethiopia's political, and financial support to African liberation struggles and leaders has been unheralded because it had to be kept secret for fear of antagonizing powerful colonial powers. The Emperor was, in all these efforts, at the helm catalyzing and leading able and committed officials and officers.

His legacy of developing the durable and respected international image of Ethiopia endures.

Emperor Haile Selassie was an individual who was proud of his country and strove to make her people proud of her. He had good reasons to feel so. He savored and nurtured a history attained and manifested by events and personalities of the past. The heritages of Lalibela, Gondar, Adulis, Magdala, Adwa, Aksum etc. and even the defeat at Maichew made him and his generation conscious of their responsibility to preserve the rich heritage and historical past. He promoted the notion that there was one historic Ethiopia, in which all the people, regardless of tribal or ethnic origin, were nationals and to which they gave their allegiance. To promote this notion of unity and consolidate his hold, the Emperor, who himself had a multi-ethnic ancestry, encouraged marriages of his children and grandchildren across tribal divides. He successfully contained ethnic rivalries and reinforced, what Erlich calls "Ethiopian awareness."

To explain his fight with General Aman, even Colonel Mengistu Haile Mariam claimed that he feared the General supported the Eritrean opposition and he could hand over "the country Haile Selassie united to bandits."[47]

Many have over the years lauded the Emperor for his leadership as well as criticized him for his failings. When it was fashionable not to speak kindly of him, they have expressed admiration for him and for his achievements. Ullendorf's admiring assertion that "there will not arise in Ethiopia anyone quite in his image"[48] or Harold Marcus' assessment that "To the last, Haile Selassie remained a humane Christian and a true Ethiopian patriot, unwilling to spill his compatriot's blood even for the sake of his empire. We shall not see his like again,"[49] might sound exaggerated, but, in many respects, the statements are true. Emperor

---

47   Anbese Ayele, Genet. *Recollections of Colonel Mengistu Haile Mariam*, Meta Publishing, Addis Ababa, 2002 pp.152-153.

48   Haile Selassie I. *My Life and Ethiopia's Progress 1892-1937.* Translation and Annotation by Ullendorf, Edward, Oxford University Press, 1976, post script XV.

49   Getachew, Indrias. *Beyond The Throne*, Addis Ababa: Shama Books, 2001, p.9.

Haile Selassie's success in meeting the challenges of his time was solid and exceptional. The towering role he played with limited means at his disposal and great odds stacked against him will indeed be difficult to match.

It is not only individuals who made up a long roster of his admirers. Emperor Haile Selassie was Time Magazine's Man of the Year in 1935 and the international media generally treated him with empathy during and after the Italo-Ethiopian War. The New York Times recognized him by including him among the fifty great lives of the twentieth century, crediting the Emperor with "leading a largely illiterate, rural, and feudal country with 2000 languages and dialects into the 19th, if not, the 20th century."[50] Over twenty prestigious institutions have conferred on him honorary degrees and he has been awarded over 100 medals from governments and organizations.[51] He had dealt with and gained the respect and admiration of the great leaders of his time. Even after his overthrow, those who were familiar of the events of the Italian occupation and the Emperor's international stature hardly bought the evil incarnate image of him the military painted. Foreigners, especially those of the older generation who have known him or know about him, saw a valiant leader who tried to bring his country into a modern era despite internal entrenched conservatism, powerful divisive forces, and colonialist designs. Haile Selasie "made greater strides toward opening the country to modern influence than all of his predecessors."[52]

These admirers knew him as a young Regent visiting Europe, knew of his historic speech in the League of Nations, closely worked with him in post-war Ethiopia, and saw his triumphs and defeats. They admired the "diminutive" politician who withstood humiliating exile with dignity and who outfoxed the British political and military post-war

---

50 Gelb, Arthur ed, Whitman, Alden. Haile Selassie 1892-1975, *Great Lives of The Twentieth Century*, Times Books, 1988, pp.250-252.

51 Kebede, Berihun. *The History of Atse Haile Selassie*, Artistic Printing Enterprise, Addis Ababa, 2000, p.28.

52 Hance, W. A. *The Geography of Modern Africa*, Columbia University press, 1964, p.351.

maneuvers. They respected and admired the leader who, with wisdom and determination, overcame the devious efforts to balkanize Ethiopia. "In 1941, Ethiopia's nationalist movement in the modern sense was in fact Emperor Haile Selassie in person. Almost all the "big men" of the time were still affiliated with provincial parochialism and interests. The Emperor, in contrast aided by a still-tiny group of modern-educated young men he had formed, was long active, motivated by a strong all-Ethiopian vision, in an effort to create a modern centralized state."[53]

Although critical of the slowness in the pace of development and of the lack of democratization, many educated Ethiopians of the post-war generation have also given him credit for the reforms he tried or engineered and the respected international status he attained for Ethiopia. Successive governments have not yet demonstrated more effective and wise leadership than he provided. Whatever positive contributions they have made, the Dergue's brutal rule has exacted a heavy price on Ethiopians while the EPRDF's divisive and ethnicity-oriented policy invites discord and disunity.

The Emperor should be, and is criticized for his failures and shortcomings, but he should be given, and he has increasingly been given by objective critics, credit for his many positive contributions to lay the foundations for the progress of Ethiopia. One cannot ignore the fact that the Emperor has, during a half a century of leadership, greatly influenced the history and progress of Ethiopia and the lives of Ethiopians of his time and of generations that followed. The goodwill, respect, and recognition his government attained for Ethiopia on the international stage still enable us to hold our heads high.

Even the devastating image of famine, the atrocities and chaotic rule of the military regime and the controversial policies of the present regime could only undermine, not destroy, the empathy and goodwill he got for Ethiopia over decades of tactful diplomacy and public relations.

Sight should not also be lost of the fact that the achievements during

---

53 Erlich, Haggai. *Ethiopia and the Challenge of Independence*. Boulder, Colorado: Lynne Reiner Publishers Inc, 1986, p.168.

his leadership were the results of the efforts of many outstanding persons who, often as initiators of change, served with him. He led a government comprised of individuals from a variety of backgrounds, different ethnic groups, from among the rich and poor. Most of the officials in the cabinet were educated and brought up during his reign and to many of them he was their mentor. Many of the top leadership were graduates of institutions of higher learning in Europe and the United States.

This generation produced elite ace pilots, able officers and men who distinguished themselves in Korea and Congo, accomplished diplomats and international civil servants, excellent doctors, and distinguished academics in higher institutions abroad. It produced pioneer writers, artists, historians, athletes who left enduring works for which they were recognized at home and abroad. Internally, this generation of leaders promoted a culture of unity among all Ethiopians, provided governance with less corruption than its successors, and ensured security and territorial integrity. The positive and consistent leadership of the Emperor made possible the emergence of a small nucleus motivated by patriotism – one that significantly contributed to the cause of progress, change, and betterment.

The generation that served under Haile Selassie has, until recently kept too silent in defending its record of service and accepting responsibility for failures. It was, and to some extent it still is, in vogue to condemn the Emperor and his rule, and, this in turn, had created an intimidating environment for those who served with him. They have, in recent writings, fortunately started setting the record straight with their more informed and balanced assessments.

While recognizing civil agitation contributed to the weakening of the monarchy and government, Ottaways give credit to this group when they wrote:

> "In hindsight it can be said that if there was any attempt to make a revolution in early 1974, it was led by urban-based educated elite and entrepreneurial bourgeoisie seeking to establish parliamentary democracy, not by

workers and students trying to establish a dictatorship of
the proletariat."[54]

In his inspiring An Album of Memories, Personal Histories from the
Greatest Generation, Tom Brokaw explores how Americans who came
of age in the Great Depression contributed to the building of America.
He calls this generation the "Greatest Generation" and enables them
to tell their stories of contributions to America's development, security,
and global role.[55] Though we hope Ethiopia's greatest generation is yet
to come, we also have our unsung achievers in traditional community
leaders, resistance fighters, politicians, soldiers, civil servants and
professional service providers who under Haile Selassie's leadership
and, despite limited resources, played their part with distinction and
wisdom in laying the foundations for unity and development.

Still, the Emperor fell victim to the common mistake of failing to
recognize that the time has come for him to phase out. Concerned
associates pleaded or advised him to delegate power to respond
to changing demands and times. Their pressure did not go beyond
some polite recommendations for change and transfer of power and
warnings of impending turbulence. Thus, their greatest failure was
their inability to do the one thing that could have enabled the Emperor
to end his days peacefully and perhaps spared the country bloodshed
and convulsions. Sidelining him with honor would have been the most
important last service they could have rendered him. The constraints
of his advancing age alone could have justified his honorable but forced
retirement. The Emperor and his close associates paid a high price for
this failure. So did Ethiopia that lost so many of its sons and daughters
and went through the reign of terror of the Mengistu years.

---

54 Ottaways, Marlina and David, *Ethiopia: Empire in Revolution*, African Publishing Company,
    1978, p.29.
55 Tom Brokaw, *An Album of Memories, Personal Histories from the Greatest Generation*, Random
    House, New York, 2001.

Vintage Haile Selassie

It is reported that when the officers informed him of his deposition and took him away, he said:

"We have carefully listened to what you said. If you have the good interest of the country, one cannot give greater priority to self-interest over the benefit to the country. We have served our country and people to the best of our abilities. If you say it is now your turn, so be it. But safeguard Ethiopia."[56]

The Emperor also warned that the Dergue should pay special attention to handling the Eritrean issue to sustain the territorial integrity of Ethiopia. The Dergue's militaristic approach and EPRDF's rash and pro-Eritrean agenda instead paved the way for Eritrea's quick cessation and encouraged some ethnic groups to talk of cessation and discriminate Ethiopians who come to work in their regions as foreigners.

The graceful, fearless, and dignified departure from power was vintage Haile Selassie. Even the officer leading the admittedly nervous group of soldiers said their "heart was touched."[57] The Emperor should have ended with what he said in the League of Nations:

"God and history will observe as witness the judgment you will give."[58]

Recent more balanced reflections on the Emperor's achievements and role attest to the fact that this prediction is coming true. His rule is increasingly judged on the basis of facts and in the light of his successors, shortcomings, the consequent turbulence, and loss of lives and ethnic tensions. Still, the governments that followed him have denied him and his associates the credit they deserve. The Dergue vindictively renamed hospitals, roads, schools, the etc. that had been built, in some cases with the Emperor's own money, and named after

---

56 Anbese, Genet Ayele, *Recollection of Colonel Mengistu Haile Mariam*, Mega Publishing Press, Addis Ababa, 1994 p.23.

57 Ibid.

58 Italy's War Crimes in Ethiopia (1935-1941),. Emperor Haile Selassie's speech at the League of Nations, June 30,1936, 2000 edition , p.83.

him. The former Haile Selassie I University is now the Addis Ababa University. The case of Tafari Makonnen School, now called Entoto Comprehensive High School, is another example. Entoto is the name of a hill in an area of the same name. In defiance, most people still address the school and its environs by its original name, Tafari Makonnen. Its decisions did not even spare the reminders of patriots who had distinguished themselves in the service of their country.

The EPRDF, though less demonizing, continued its subtle defamation of the Emperor and his government. It maintained the Dergue's charges and continued to belittle reminders of the historical past and times. Ethiopian leaders need to take note that a country's historical past is a heritage that should not be wiped out by fiat of those in power and their shortsighted political decisions.

Initiatives to recognize the Emperor's service and contributions have been launched by establishing non-profit organizations and programs in his name in and outside the country. The principal one is the Haile Selassie Humanitarian Foundation, which awards scholarships and plans to build libraries. No doubt there will be other initiatives in the future. Hopefully, a proposal, encouraged by General Firesenbet Amde to convert the former Jubilee Palace to a national museum, would eventually materialize. A study is reportedly under way to assess how this could be done. The Imperial souvenirs and valuable belongings reflect part of the country's past and they should be treasured, as it is done in other countries, properly for the benefit of posterity.

Such actions and initiatives would recognize and help reflect the history of the Haile Selassie years. However, and more importantly, the legacy of the Emperor is enshrined in the minds of those who believe in the oneness and unity of the Ethiopian people, in the indivisibility of the country, and in a responsible role in the international arena. The Emperor and his associates lived for and advanced these sublime goals and reposed the trust in those who follow to refine and further their fulfillment.

Bibliography

Alemayehu, Haddis. *Tizita*. Addis Ababa: Kuraz Publishing Agency, 1992.

Abogne (Abdosh), Abdullah. *Bercha: Cryptic Tales of Harar & Glimpses of My Life*. Addis Ababa: Artistic Printing Press, 2003.

Anbese, Genet Ayele. *Recollections of Colonel Mengistu Haile Mariam*. Addis Ababa: Mega Publishing Press, 1994.

Belette, Haile Ghiorghis, *The History of Ras Makonnen*, Completed in Geez in 1938 Etc. Trans. Kinfe Gabriel Altaye. Commercial Printing Press, 1996.

Brokaw, Tom. *The Greatest Generation*, New York: Random House, 1998""*"An Album of Memories, Personal Histories from the Greatest Generation*, New York: Random House, 2001

Caraman, Philip. *The Lost Empire, The Story of the Jesuits in Ethiopia 1555-1634*, Notre Dame: University of Notre Dame, Press, 1985.

Diggins, John P. *Mussolini And Fascism*. Princeton: Princeton University Press, Princeton, 1972.

Erlich, Haggai. *Ethiopia And The Challenge of Independence*, Boulder, Lynne Reinner Publishers: 1986.

Gebru, Dawit, *Kentiba Gebru Desta*. Addis Ababa: Bole Printing Press, 1993.

Getachew, Indrias. *Beyond The Throne*. Addis Ababa: Shamma Books, 2001.

Gelb, Arthur ed, Whitman, Alden. *Haile Selassie ,1892-1975. Great Lives of the Twentieth Century.* New York, New York Times Books, 1988.

Haile Selassie. *My Life and Ethiopia's Progress.* Addis Ababa: Berhanena Selam Printing Press, 1958.

Haile Selassie Teferra. *The Ethiopian Revolution 1974-1991: From a Monarchical to a Military Oligarchy.* London and New York: Kegan Paul International, 1997.

Haile Selassie I Memorial Foundation. *Special Issue on The 112th. Birthday of Emperor.* Adddis Ababa: July, 2004.

Hance, W.A. *The Geography of Modern Africa.* New York: Columbia University Press, 1994.

Habte Wold, Aklilu. *Historical Diary And Notes Written in Prison.* Addis Ababa: Tobia, Vol. 2, 1994.

Hawarya. Vol.1, No. 18.

Ethiopian Holocaust Remembrance Committee. *Italy's War Crimes in Ethiopia (1935-1941). Ethiopian Holocaust Remembrance Committee,*2000.

Jones A.H. & Monroe E. *The History of Abyssinia*, Oxford: Oxford University Press, 1935.

Kebede, Berihun. *The History of Atse Haile Selassie*, Addis Ababa: Artistic Printing Press, September 28, 2000 .

Lee, Helene. *The First Rasta*, France: Flammarion, 1999.

Lockot, Hans Wilhelm. *The Mission: The Life, Reign And Character of Haile Selassie*, New York : ECA Associates Press, USA, New York 1993.

Mandela, Nelson. *Long Walk To Freedom*, USA: Little, Brown and Company, 1994.

Mengesha Haile Mariam. *Mot Amba Derso Mels* (translation: Return from Death Village). Addis Ababa, Commercial Printing Press, 1987.

Sandford, Christine. *Ethiopia Under Haile Selassie.* London: J.M.Dent & Sons, Ltd., 1946.

Ottaway, Marina and David. *Empire in Revolution .USA:* Africana Publishing Company, 1978.

Scott William R. *The Sons of Sheba's Race. Bloomington:* Indiana University Press, 1993.

The Report of The Education Sector Review, *Education: Challenge To The Nation.* Addis Ababa, 1972.

Wolde Maryam, Dehne. *Unpublished Diary*, Asinara, 1937.

Starkie, Enid, *Arthur Rimbaud.* New York: New Directions Books, 1961

Ullendorf, Edward, translated and annotated by. *The Autobiography of Emperor Haile Selassie I: 'My Life and Ethiopia's Progress' 1892-1937*. USA: Oxford University Press, 1976.

Wikipedia, The Free Encyclopedia. *Ras Tafari Movement:The Selassie Visit to Jamaica*, 1966.

Wolde Giorgis, Ayalew. *In the Palace of Emperor Haile Selassie*. USA, Southern Heritage Press, 2002.

Yifru, Ketema. *Letter dated July 1971* and read at Memorial July 1994.